# MASS COMMUNICATION TODAY

# MASS COMMUNICATION TODAY

**Urmila Devi**

ACE BOOKS INDIA

NEWDELHI

**ACE Books India**
4649-B/21, Ansari Road
Darya Ganj, New Delhi - 110 002

*Mass Communication Today*



First Published 2010
ISBN 978-81-909743-1-8



*Sole Distributors*
**EKTA BOOKS DISTRIBUTORS**
4649-B/21, Ansari Road
Darya Ganj, New Delhi - 110 002
Ph.: 23263193 / 9811582579 / 09435116718
Fax: 011-23263193
Email: ektabooks@yahoo.com
www.akanshapublishinghouse.com

PRINTED IN INDIA

Published by ACE Books India, New Delhi and Printed at
**Harmain Offset Press**

# Contents


| | | |
|---|---|---|
| | *Preface* | *vii* |
| 1. | Mass Communication: What, Why and How? | 1 |
| 2. | The Nature of Mass Communication | 42 |
| 3. | Theoretical Approaches to Communication | 69 |
| 4. | The Communications Revolution | 121 |
| 5. | Professional Organization of Mass Communicators | 148 |
| 6. | Audio-Visual Revolution | 176 |
| 7. | Mass Communication and MIS | 214 |
| | *Appendix* | 239 |
| | *Glossary* | 261 |
| | *Bibliography* | 278 |
| | *Index* | 281 |

# Preface

> "Precepts or maxims are of great weight; and a few useful ones at hand do more toward a happy life than whole volumes that we know not where to find."
>
> —*Seneca*

Basically, 'Mass communication' consists of two terms—'mass' and 'communication'. While the term 'mass' suggests that the recipients of media products constitute a vast sea of passive, undifferentiated individuals. This is an image associated with some earlier critiques of 'mass culture' and mass society which generally assumed that the development of mass communication has had a largely negative impact on modern social life, creating a kind of bland and homogeneous culture which entertains individuals without challenging them.

On the other hand, the aspect of 'communication' refers to the giving and taking of meaning, the transmission and reception of messages. The word 'communication' is really equated with 'transmission', as viewed by the sender, rather than in the fuller meaning, which includes the notions of response, sharing and interaction. Messages are produced by one set of individuals and transmitted to others who are typically situated in settings that are spatially and temporally remote from the original context of production. Therefore, the term 'communication' in this context masks the social and industrial nature of the media, promoting a tendency to think of them as interpersonal communication. Furthermore, it is known that recipients today do have some capacity to intervene in and contribute to the course and content of the communicative process.

They are being both active and creative towards the messages that they are conveyed of. With the complement of the cyberspace supported by the Internet, not only that recipients are participants in a structured process of symbolic transmission, constraints such as time and space are reordered and eliminated.

Thus, 'Mass communication' can be seen as institutionalized production and generalized diffusion of symbolic goods via the fixation and transmission of information or symbolic content. It is known that the systems of information codification has shifted from analog to digital. This has indeed advanced the communication between individuals. With the existence of Infrared, Bluetooth and Wi-Fi, cell phones are no longer solely a tool for audio transmission. We can transfer photos, music documents or even games and email at any time and anywhere. The development of media technology has indeed advanced the transmission rate and stability of information exchange.

However, with the advancement in Media Technology, people are no longer receiving gratification without questioning the grounds on which it is based.

Instead, people are engaging themselves more with media products such as computers, cell phones and Internet. These have gradually became vital tools for communications in society today.

Further, the academic mass communication discipline historically differs from media studies and communication studies programs with roots in departments of theatre, film or speech, and with more interest in "qualitative," interpretive theory, critical or cultural approaches to communication study. In contrast, many mass communication programs historically lean toward empirical analysis and quantitative research — from statistical content analysis of media messages to survey research, public opinion polling, and experimental research.

Interest in "New Media" and "Computer Mediated Communication" is growing much faster than educational institutions can assimilate it. So far, traditional classes and degree programs have not been able to accommodate new shifts of the paradigm in communication technologies.

Mass communication is the term used to describe the academic study of the various means by which individuals and entities relay information through mass media to large segments of the population at the same time. It is usually understood to relate to newspaper and magazine publishing, radio, television and film, as these are used both for disseminating news and for advertising.

This volume contains valuable information on mass communication. All salient features are given elaborate treatment in systematic and scientific way. Major topics dealt in this include—Mass Communication: What, Why and How?; The Nature of Mass Communication; Theoretical Approaches to Communication; The Communications Revolution; Professional Organization of Mass Communicators; Audio-Visual Revolution; Communication Mass and MIS; Appendices; Glossary; and Bibliography etc.

In fact, this book is devised as a dependable reference handbook for media persons. So the text is supported by well-researched readings, penned by leading experts in the field. Real credit for this ought go to them all. I am deeply beholden to all original contributors, their publishers and sources for subscribing their views. My friends and colleagues have helped me a lot while working on this. I am grateful to them all. Finally, I am thankful to my publisher for bringing out this in elegant manner within shortest possible time.

We will appreciate if the learned readers could communicate us their comments and suggestions for the improvement in utility of this, which we may incorporate in the subsequent edition of the book.

—**Author**

# 1

# Mass Communication: What, Why and How?

> "The best advice I can give to any young man or young woman upon graduation from school can be summed up in exactly eight words, and they are—be honest with yourself and tell the truth."
>
> —*James A. Farley*

Basically, Communication is derived from Latin word 'communico' which means sharing and not just sending messages. Therefore, communication is a social process, and countless ways in which human beings keep in touch with one another. The communication may be verbal, non-verbal, written, audio-visual etc. The act of communication suggests a sender (of message), receiver. The message is what is communed between the two. The message is shared, reacted, non-reacted. When there is active communication, the effort is for interaction, interchange, dialogue and mutual understanding. Communication presupposes a shared symbolic environment, a social relationship among those who participate, leading to social interaction. The messages in the shared environment could not only be oral, non-verbal, written, visual, olfactory; but these could be laws, customs, practices, ways of dressing, gestures, buildings, gardens, exhibits, flags etc.

Language and body synthesizers which are culture specific are essential components of messages. People in communication define the various types of society, sub-society and groups. Their characteristics depend upon the modes of communication they possess, media usage, rituals and signs of personal relationships. The traditional concepts of communication is that we use communication to express our inner purposes, attitudes, feelings, and to describe events and objects of the external world; to produce 'sharedness' between the speaker and the audience addressed. Another view is that patterns of social communication constitute the world as we know. It is a primary social process.

Notably Pearce (1989) presents the premise that we live in communication rather than outside of communication and use communication for our own purposes. In the era of communication revolution, communication is far more important and central for human condition than ever before realised. There is recognition that multiple forms of communication exist in contemporary human society. These forms are not neutral. They are alternative forms of being human. Each qualitatively different form of communication affords a particular array of opportunities and problems. To communicate actively or passively is one of the basic needs. We talk of basic minimum needs of foods, clothing, shelter, education and health. But 'right to communicate' whether actively or passively is the essential basic social needs. Human beings cannot survive without communicating.

Communication is the locus of forces through which persons create and manage social realities. Social reality includes concept of self, community, institutions and cultures. Through communication we create conceptions of SELF—

who we are; we create relationships within the community and build institutions. We communicate and act together to create, recreate community relationships. Relationships exist and are managed within a culture. Human communication notion is not always getting the accuracy of transmission but of social reality creation.

It is significant to note that the concept of communication has been continuously revised. There is a clear direction in these revisions. They have consistently shown communication to be subtle, complex, and complicated process. In a judgment these revisions are fully warranted but insufficiently radical. They are piecemeal attempts to patch up flawed notion of communication. The revisions retain the assumptions that communication is a subset of human actions or situations and the task of a definition (of communication) is to differentiate a category of events/objects that comprise communication from those that do not. The propensity to differentiate communication from not communication follows one of Aristotle's laws of identity. In contemporary thought, the Aristotelian heritage is expressed in the assumption that one communicates only by speaking, reading, writing or by using sign language but not by sleeping, eating or running. There is little difficulty in identifying a particular instance of social action as communication. The problem arises in specifying what human actions are not communication. It is impossible to identify a set of 'critical attributes' to differentiate between communication and that which is not communication.

Any form of social action can be shown to be communication. But it may be argued that communication is better understood as a perspective or context from which any act may be examined and understood. It is not that communication occurs by speaking rather than sleeping, by listening rather than walking away or by broadcasting a radio programme rather than burning a bus. One may communicate eloquently by sleeping-students do it in large lecture classes. One may communicate by walking away, subjects sometimes do when ask for an interview. The assumption is that any action has message value. One cannot NOT communicate. Whatever one does or does not do CAN BE looked at from a 'communication perspective'.

From the communication perspective human actions are seen as the process by which persons collectively maintain social reality. Human beings simultaneously live in a symbolic universe (social reality) and with other people. They actively strive to create coherent stories drawing from the 'resources' of their social reality and from the practices in which they are engaged with others. They tell themselves stories that explain and guide their performance in practices and they enact stories that exemplify and 'test' their resources. Implications are that communication perspective facilitate interpretative and critical analysis. The result of this sort of analysis is that meanings of actions, both of one's own and others are made transparent and increases the possibility of communication. Thus from this perspective, many social actions that otherwise would not be defined as instances of communication are shown to be powerful means of creating and managing a social reality. For example consider public works and legislation; from communication perspective both powerfully expressed and construct the social realities of the masses and the government themselves.

Remarkably, Pearce (1989) argues that there are two issues: One, is the difficulty of achieving satisfactory widely accepted definition of communication; Second, is our ability to offer any definition. The problem occurs in two contexts.

One context is our public discourse both among ourselves and other colleagues in the discipline. A review of literature from 1955 onwards suggests a futile attempt to produce a definition of communication which would serve as a disciplinary basis on which research, teaching and services could be grounded; rather it has landed in for 'family' of concepts. Pearce further argues that the other context is of friends and relatives.

It is hard to explain communication to friends and relatives because they *do not differentiate themselves* sufficiently from communication per se. Without a formal study it is difficult to see *What* you say as incarnation of a larger system of beliefs and values; the *style* of what you say as enmeshed in existing systems; and the *implications* of what you say as regularly and normally proceeding from unacknowledged constraints and leading to unanticipated consequences. We talk of communication as it is something 'outside' us and as if our talk of communication is something other than we are talking about. It is hard to explain communication to ourselves precisely for the opposite reason. We differentiate ourselves too much from communication per se.

In fact communication has been subjected to numerous and diverse conceptualisations. However, the key features of most definitions are:

(a) Communication is persuasive and seeks to obtain desirable response to what is being transmitted.

(b) Human communication is a process of transmission of ideas, thoughts, feelings and behaviour from one person to another person.

(c) Communication is a multiway process, two-way process.

### Basic Elements

Now, let us see how our daily activities involve communication. We may talk to a person, write a letter, interview, show/watch a film of slide, prepare a write up or a pamphlet, organise an exhibition, carry out a demonstration, participate in radio, T.V. programmes—thus we are engaged in a communication process. In essence communication means sharing of ideas between/among persons using verbal, visual, and written symbols.

Practically, there are several elements in the communication process. To generate communication we need five basic elements: source, message, channel, receiver and effect of message. *Who say what. With what purpose. To whom. In what situation. By what means. With what effect.*

### Who?

The communicator is the source of the message that he delivers to the people. The communicator can be the primary or secondary source of message. When he is secondary source of message he may get the information from other source who is more knowledgeable about the message. But it is the responsibility of the communicator to communicate it to the people in the form they can understand easily. To make communication effective, communicator must know the characteristics of the receiver/audience.

A good knowledge of audience—their socio-cultural background, their needs, their problems, their limitations and level of comprehension will help the communicator to design an effective message. Source credibility is essential for effective communication. The communicator must have faith in what he is communicating; as well his audience must have faith in the communicator. Therefore, it is essential that the communicator must have adequate knowledge, information on the topic that he is communicating about. Moreover, he must have the communication skills to convey the message in effective way. Thus source credibility can be generated by communication skills of the communicator, his information and knowledge about the topic of communication.

**The Objective**

The communicator must be clear about the response from the audience. What exactly he wants them to do. His communication efforts will most likely be directed to informing, educating, reasoning and legitimating. The effectiveness of communication will depend upon the ability to define the objectives clearly and use of appropriate communication techniques to achieve the objectives.

**The Audience**

Communication requires receivers and consumers of messages, the 'people' with whom he communicates. A communicator must know his audience characteristics in general and specifically. The audience's characteristics, their background, past experience, learning abilities, interests, attitudes, and values etc. can affect their receptiveness to the messages conveyed as well as effectiveness of the messages. When you say that your audience consists of farm families, you are taking in general terms. But then farm people are not a homogeneous group.

The individuals in the group differ in their educational background, level of income, cultural social background, language, world of experience, and points of contact. These individuals may comprise the specific farm groups. A specific group may be the targeted audience. Therefore to communicate effectively, it is necessary not only to know the general audience characteristics but also to know the specific audience. If the audience is clearly defined and its characteristics known, it will be easier for the communicator to put across the message.

**In What Situation?**

The situation in which you are reaching the audience will affect the response. It makes a difference whether you are vising a person in his home, office, in a meeting, in a large gathering or in the market place. The place, time, the relationships of the group members etc. create the communication environment. The effectiveness of any message will depend on the communication environment in which it is being conveyed or received. The communication environment may be conducive, hostile, appropriate or inappropriate. The environment is hostile if communicator is talking about family planning to a group who are hostile to the idea of family planning. People in a slum colony wants to self-rely on cleanliness of the colony. The message of cleanliness will be received by them in a conducive environment.

**By What Means?**

Communication of ideas through the spoken word is described by various-terms—face to face communication, interpersonal communication, person to person contact or word of mouth communication. This is the oldest and still the most effective among the various communication channels. You need a channel, a carrier, a medium to communicate with your audience. You can regard it as a vehicle that takes your message to the audience and their response to you. In many traditional societies for centuries, the spoken word has been the main means of communicating ideas.

The second medium is non-verbal communication channels. Through body gestures, expressions, non-verbal acts the message is conveyed. When the mob burns the bus, the commuters are conveying their hostility and discontent for the transit system. If a student sleeps through the class lectures he is communicating his boredom perhaps. The written word has come to play an important role in communicating today. The written message is used in many forms—posters, charts, blackboard, leaflets, wall newspaper, news stories, circular letters, pamphlets and flyers, besides the newspapers, magazines, and books. Low rate of literacy can constraint the use of written communication. Another mode of communication is through pictures. A picture is a symbol of real object. Pictures can be used in many forms to communicate, such as illustrations, posters, photographs, exhibits, slides, filmstrips, films and models. While some pictures are self-explanatory, others require use of written words. It is easier to convey ideas through pictures because they are more precise than spoken or written words. You can use various combinations of three basic forms of communication—spoken, written and visuals. In many communication situations, the combinations produce better results.

When you write on the blackboard or show a chart while you speak, you combine written word with the spoken word. When you use photographs, models, slides, flannelgraph, charts and flash cards etc. while you speak to the audience you combine the spoken word with the pictures. Again when you are showing a movie you are combining spoken words with visuals. In a poster or exhibits, you combine written words with pictures. People receive messages through all five senses—sight, hearing, smell, taste and touch. The message is likely to be understood better if it appeals to more than one sense at a time.

Different forms of communication appeal to different people. For effective communication, the audience must be involved in different experiences using several sources if possible.

In fact, in our day to day life, we realise that no single channel can reach all the people we want to reach. People vary in their experiences, abilities, tastes, skills, attitudes etc. Therefore, the choice of channels depends on the characteristics of the audience. Therefore, for effective communication choose the channel to suit the audience. The experience also shows that people donot necessarily get the message in one single exposure. Repeated exposures of the messages through variety of channels will reinforce the message and be effective. At the same time saturation point both for message exposure as well as channel exposure must be avoided. Since messages become ineffective at the saturation point.

It must be remembered that one single channel cannot be used to reach all kinds of audiences as well as to communicate all types of messages. Therefore, a communicator must know what channel will work better for what type of messages and what kind of audience. Accordingly he will choose his message and channel to reach his targeted audience. A communicator may use one or several channels depending upon the nature of the message or the targeted audience.

The message may have to be reinforced through different channels at the same time or at different point of time to ensure that it reaches the audience effectively. Changing people's attitude and behaviour is a slow process. This kind of change cannot be produced by exposing the audience once. It will require a systemic approach of extensive and intensive message exposures and reinforcements and channel mix over a period of time to achieve the desired communication effects. Therefore, for effective communication, appropriate channel should be selected as well use appropriately.

**What?**

The communicator must define the contents of the message and be clear about them. The contents may be information, ideas, attitude appeal etc. There must be something useful to say, something which the communicator wants the people to understand and act upon. Before deciding the exact message and an effective message; a communicator must be affirmative about the following message elements:

(a) Will it help the audience improve their knowledge or skill or both to do a specific job that they need to do.

(b) Does the audience need this message.

(c) Has the message (ideas) been tried before and found useful and profitable.

(d) Has it been recommended by appropriate authorities.

(e) Is your message specific.

(f) Is your information accurate, precise and exact.

(g) Is the information update and timely.

(h) Is the idea compatible with the existing socio-cultural conditions in which they live and work.

(i) Is audience equipped to take the message.

Notably only such messages that pass this test will be received, acted upon and provide the audience and communicator satisfaction. Message is a set of CODES that has its own meaning to the communicator and receiver. The code could be verbal, non-verbal, or written. Message has a CONTENT or theme. It has a STYLE which is reflective of culture, sub-culture, geographic area and contexts involved. The effectiveness and responsiveness to the message depends on its presentation (style). Sometimes the stereotype presentation may overkill the effectiveness of the message.

**With What Effect?**

Basically, main purpose of any communication programme is to produce an impact on a certain audience. The impact of any communication efforts can be assessed in relation to the objective of the communication act. There may not be any active communication unless there is dynamic inter-play of source, message, channel and audience to produce an EFFECT. If you observe your audience carefully in inter-personal communication situation, you can find out from their reactions, expressions, actions and comments whether they are interested, clear, bored or confused about your message. This kind of feedback is helpful in adjusting your message or channel to make it more interesting or purposeful. This kind of short-term effect on the audience is clear indication of the long-term impact of your message. The short-term effect of communication is judged by the change is has produced in people's knowledge, attitude, behaviour and skill. The long-term effect of communication is assessed by people's actions.

Communication effects have two basic components: *Information processing and levels of communication effect evaluation.*

When an individual receive messages, what happens? To start with there is a selective exposure and selective perception on the part of the entity towards whom the messages are directed. Selective exposure is tendency to attend to communication messages that are consistent with the entity's existing needs, attitudes and beliefs. Selective perception, on the other hand is the tendency to interpret communication messages in terms of receiver's needs, attitudes and beliefs. Following selective exposure and perception, the person starts assimilating the thematic content and acceptance and rejection of the information received. There is high probability of information being utilised if the information is consistent with receiver's attitudes, beliefs and rationality.

When we say 'communication is successful' or 'communication has failed', these are evaluated questions related to communication effects. Evaluation is done at three stages: (a) stage of transmission, (b) stage of semantics, (c) stage of effectiveness. Let us take example of effective communication about rural bank loans.

At the first level, we evaluate the success of communication by rural bank officer by examining whether people have physically received the message about bank loans.

At the second level, we examine whether people have understood the received information in the same way as bank officer has intended to convey and wants them to understand.

Thirdly, it is not just sufficient to make sure that people have properly understood the communication content but that the bank officer/rural banking agency would be expecting from people is a change in their values, attitudes and behaviour. The ultimate aim being to motivate people to take practical actions of the communication content. If the final objective of the communication is met, we say communication is effective; otherwise either there is communication failure or communication gap.

Several factors contribute towards communication success at each level of communication. At the level of transmission factors such as media distribution, media capacity, media accessibility (both physical and social), media scheduling etc.; and resources and accessibility of interpersonal communication channels contribute in ensuing transmission of communication messages. At the level of semantics, the CODE and STYLE used in message formulation are crucial. At the effectiveness stage, audience formation processing behaviour, culture, tradition and other development inputs contribute in behavioural changes. To ensure communication success, the commentator resorts to reinforcement of messages by repeated exposures, by detailed explanation (education) of the messages. Motivation is another intervention used by the communicator to gain communication success. Motivation can range from simple persuasion to incentives through an educational process.

Homophily between the source and the target audience can contribute to successful communication. Homophily is defined as the degree to which source-receiver pair is similar in certain attributes like beliefs, education, social status etc. Source credibility as held by the audience is another factor contributing towards communication success. Many times communication fails because of 'information over kill' (very familiar characteristics of message formulations) or by 'information overload'!

**Feedback**

In fact, communication is not static. It is a process of sending messages and messages being received. S→M→C→R→E model (source-message-channel-receiver-effect) is a linear model and suggests unidirectional flow of communication from source to audience. There is no exchange of communication messages and as such how can this be called communication? At the most we can call this as dissemination of information of messages. The moment we have exchange of ideas and experiences—we have communication. We can have two-way communication, multiways communication process by having dialogue and multilogues. The assumptions is that receiver is not passive, he must react to the message that he receives. Thus the communication situation allows *feedback* from the audience to the source.

Notably, purpose of feedback is numerous. The audience would like to express their point of view or thoughts in response to stimulation from the source; or the audience may like to have clarification of certain point put forth by the source; or the source itself may encourage audience to provide feedback to its communication strategies so as to improve or modify the ensuing communication strategies. The feedback whether it is immediate or delayed is useful in view of the fact that the communication situation is no longer unidirectional but ensures interaction between the systems or entities.

With or without feedback, the S→M→C→R→E model is a linear model. But communication is not always one step flow as it often looks, several entities come in between the source and the targeted audience. This calls for interactive communication among the members of a communication group. Thus with several loops of feedback communication becomes a process of reaction and action to what is said. By acting and interacting we create patterns and we create communication.

### Feedback in Mass Media

Feedback to media systems from audience is mainly through readers/viewers mail. Audience research, surveys etc. Whatever their form, the massmediated communication is different from unmediated communication as far as feedback and role taking is concerned.

There may be feedback through readers, viewers, listeners mail, audience research, ratings etc. but in immediate sense very little feedback exists for mass media systems. The communicator has no ongoing cues as the message is being delivered. In turn audience has little control over the content, structure or pace of media presentation. Thus mass communication is only linear and one way process and in order that it should be effective correct role taking and feedback process have to be built into the system.

In the absence of these the audience may interpret mediated messages in distorted ways. The feedback through the audience mail is of two categories: (a) mail directly or indirectly related with the functioning of mass media systems. It is audience reaction to definite material—the programme content, policies etc.; (b) mail of personal character comprising, requests or seeking advice. This way also draw attention of the media to public problems of common significance. The latter writers think they are intermediate link between the media and the audience. Mass media may invite the audience to participate in discussions, readers' conferences etc.

Thus by giving feedback through mail, the audience expresses public opinion, draw attention of public to common issues, raise significant issues; and stimulate for higher quality of programmes and efficiency. The major constraint of mass mediated messages is that feedback is delayed and not immediate and there is no interactive feedback.

### Feedback in Interpersonal Communication

Here it is pertinent to note that interpersonal communication is not a linear process. It is complex and dynamic. The communicator in face to face situation is alert to various verbal and non-verbal cues on the part of the receiver that provide feedback. This is taken into account as the message is formulated, and transmitted.

Feedback is essentially a reverse communication process initiated by the receiver and directed at the communicator. It may be verbal, non-verbal or both. Feedback is usually provided on an ongoing basis in such a way that it can have substantial influence on the message formulation by the communicator. Thus in face to face situation the meanings are transferred back and forth as the message of the one stimulates the other. When the communicator reduces incongruence by interpreting feedback cues correctly and adjusting message content to achieve greater effectiveness and accuracy; he or she is engaged in what Mead referred to as ROLE TAKING. Role taking is a process by which communicator assesses which configuration of meanings for given symbols will arouse parallel configurations in the experience of the receivers. Thus the greater the amount of feedback provided, the more adequate is the communicator's role taking; and less incongruence will result in communication.

Thus the process of communicator is a reciprocal one and at least partially under the control of both communicator and receivers. Effective use of feedback in interpersonal communication can be made if feedback is immediate as it reinforces the message. Feedback should be appropriate to the communication situation—specifically about the message to the speaker.

The feedback should be clear on two counts one it is feedback to the message; two it is clear in meaning. Since feedback is informative, it should convey some additional information which the speaker does not already know. Feedback about one's understanding of the message and one's agreement or disagreement about it should be honest.

## Communication Paradigms

As is obvious from the preceding discussion, the term 'communication' is difficult to define. There are some well-articulated concepts of communication which express this perspective, which might be useful as the basis for development planning which does not limit itself to linear views of communication. These include: Symbol Circulation concept, Mass-line concept, and Circular concept of communication. The Linear Paradigm treats communication as an act whereas the other three concepts define communication as a process.

***Linear Paradigm :*** One of the earliest models of communication was implied in the rhetoric of the classical Greeks, most notably by Aristotle. According to him, the speaker the speech, and the audience are the constituent elements of the communication act. The 'communicator' is the speaker, who is actively transmitting messages to a passive audience, who are not communicators, at least at present. Beltran (1976) describes this 'one way' concept of communication as a 'vertical' model and this concept is fully embedded in the currently influential models of Lasswell (1948) and Shannon and Weaver (1949). During the next decade, three other influential communication models were developed. Wilbur Schramm (1955) described communication as an act of establishing contact between a sender and receiver, with the help of a message (S→M→R model). Westley and MacLean (1957) and Berlo (1960) introduced the additional element of 'feedback' to the model. Berlo even described communication as a process, but these remained essentially linear models of one way communication and could describe the communication act and not the communication process.

The linear notion of communication was very influential in the early concepts of development. But soon the limitations of the linear models became apparent and were critiqued by development theorists as well as communication theorists. There are some 'patch' and 'repair' alternatives including the 'two step flow' (Katz and Lazarfeld, 1957; Rogers, 1969), 'multi-step flow' (Rogers, 1971, 1976) hypothesis but they do not refer to the thrust of the criticisms.

Kincaid (1979, p. 28) critiqued linear models as treating information like a physical substance and individual minds like separate entities. These assumptions have created seven biases in the study of human communication.

(i) Communication is usually a vertical, one way act rather than cyclical, two way process over time;

(iii) a source bias based on the dependency rather than on the relationship of those who communicate and their interdependency;

(iii) the objects of communication are treated as existing in a vacuum, isolated from their context;

(iv) the focus is on the message per se at the expense of silence, punctuation and timings of the message;

(v) the primary purpose of communication is considered as persuasion rather than mutual understanding, agreement and collective action;

(vi) there is concentration on the psychological effects of communication on separate individuals rather than the social effects and the relationships among individuals;

(vii) belief in one way mechanistic causation rather than mutual casuation.

In the context of development, during the 1950's and 1960's, the linear paradigm of communication had been identified with mass media communication. By its very nature the mass communication is one way flow of messages with little or no possibilities for the receivers to respond to the senders or media; it is impersonal but simultaneous. The vertical top-down interpersonal communication is identifiable with the linear model.

***Symbol Circulation Concept:*** This concept emphasises the point that the 'meaning' of development messages are interpreted by the masses and the development planners according to their specific 'symbolic environment.' This interpretation affects their actions for development. Such a concept may suggest a different communication handling for people exposed to different symbolic environments according to their social structure, social status, education, occupation and sex. This concept identifies communication as more of a process, a multivariable dynamic interplay of numerous factors, some of them quite intangible. In this view the 'meaning' is treated more as a property of the receiver than the message.

Bordenave (1972) argued that the receiver was not a blank page on which we could write our messages but a living being whose beliefs, attitudes, and values grew out of his own experience. The receiver interprets the 'messages' according to his own 'meanings,' i.e. his 'symbolic environments.' Thus it is the symbol of the message and not the message itself which is transmitted. Singh and

Gross (1979) conceptualise the symbols of development and mobilisation as part of the symbolic environment. What is transmitted depends entirely on the recipients' perception of the symbols. As messages become more complex or less routinised, the possibility of symbols being understood in one way by the sender and in many different ways by the various receivers is vastly enlarged. There are practical conclusions to be derived from these fundamental facts: one is that to be successful in communicating certain information, a sender must understand the values and biases of many different recipients.

Secondly, the sender might use entirely different symbols to convey similar messages to different audiences. Finally, the different recipients' perception of any particular set of symbols is usually affected by the extent to which and the manner in which those recipients may be involved in either the process of communication or in the activity referred to by the messages. This could be passive or active involvement. In this context, it may be useful to think that the *process* of transmitting a message and the *contents* of the message itself are usually affected by the sender's perception of the possible receivers, as well as the information the sender may receive from them during the process of transmission itself about the receipt of the message, the extent to which it may have been understood or misunderstood. This is often referred as 'feedback.' How we understand what someone says and how much we believe it to be true will subsequently influence how we act alone or in concert with others. Grunig (1968) had argued the importance of 'function' of individual social status and social structure for access to messages and media. He argues that the studies of innovation, decision-making, and information seeking behaviour in many developing countries suggested that the functions performed by various messages and media in the life of each person were different according to the position occupied by the individual in the social structure and the social structure itself is very powerful determinant of people's access to mass media.

***Mass Line Concept:*** Singh K. (1976) pointed out that Mao Tse Tung (China) identified the mass the concept of communication with the mass non-elitist leadership. Gandhi (India) endorsed Mao's viewpoint and suggested a 'bottom-up' communication between the people and the development functionaries. Singh argued that leadership of the people is identified with opinion leadership. Opinion leadership is a widely used concept in development and is relevant for interpersonal communication for development.

The argument is that people communicate their development needs and need priorities to development functionaries. This suggests that to make development plans need oriented, these should be supported by people's knowledge, wisdom, experience and judgement, however poor and illiterate they may be. This concept of communication presupposes (i) people's participation and leadership in development, and (ii) opinion leadership as a significant communication link between people and the development functionaries. The mass line concept of communication is the basis for a critique of the elitist leadership role in development identified with top-down communication, where the development planners/functionaries by their 'trained incapacity' do not learn from the masses' experience, wisdom and judgement. They thus create a gap between the social reality of the people and that of the development planners/functionaries.

***Circular Concept:*** The circular concept of communication coordinates vertical and horizontal communication, feedback and the principle of 'convergence.'

This concept identifies two dimensions of vertical communication, 'top-down' and 'bottom-up,' and a form of horizontal communication i.e. 'bottom-bottom' communication among the people. In the context of development it is envisaged that both vertical communication, i.e. from government to people, from people to government and horizontal communication, i.e. communication among the members of the development bureaucracy and among people is necessary to make the development programmes need-oriented. There has to be circular flow of communication at all levels. Kincaid's (1979) principle of convergence suggests that 'feedback' is a process and not one-half of one cycle of information exchange as advocated by the linear paradigm. An analysis of a series of such cycles of information exchange over time are necessary to understand the human communication as a process.

Convergence and divergence are useful terms for describing what actually occurs during this process. Convergence is tendency to move towards one point or one another, to come together and unite in a common interest and focus. Divergence is simply moving away or apart. The second important feature of the principle of convergence is that it presupposes the pre-existence of a goal and the feedback is positive or negative only with respect to a predetermined goal. In the context of development, the fundamental purpose of human communication is to understand reality in order to a achieve goals and select other subsequent goals. Thus understanding and mutual understanding are fundamental to the process of communication itself. A circular communication is necessary at all levels with several loops of feedback and feed forward to arrive at mutual understanding.

## Information and Communication

In fact, it may be useful to identify communication as different from information. Communication is something that happens to information but it is not information itself; though it is absolutely essential in the process of both collection and dissemination of information. The progress of any society will be affected by the type and volume of information that flows within its system. The speed and flow of communication will further depend on the urgency and importance of the matter and receptivity of the audience.

The information should be relevant, meaningful, to the knowledge and lifestyle of the people. For example development information should be adequate and timely. Such information is of two kinds: one is the information meant for the people about development plans and their operations, the other is information meant for the development bureaucracy which operates the development programmes.

## Categories

Communication occurs in many forms at different levels. These are categorised into three forms. Broad forms, Functional forms and Geographic forms. The three forms overlap and are convenient and practical categories.

***1. Broad:*** These forms of communication are Intrapersonal, Transpersonal, Interpersonal, Group Communication, Mass Communication and Folk Communication. Intrapersonal communication is communication with onself. It is individual's reflection with oneself, contemplation and meditation. Transpersonal is communication with Divine through prayers, meditation etc. Interpersonal communication is face to face communication. It could be dydic, among a smaller or larger group of people. Thus group communication is essentially interpersonal.

It could be formal like public meetings, lecture discussions and also non-formal like religious services, village markets, bazaars, melas, gossip groups, tea shop groups etc. Folk Communication also called Traditional or popular media can be both interpersonal, group or mediated. The communication is through folk channels of songs, dance, theatre, religious discourses and mass religious meetings like Bhajans, Jagratas and Satsang etc. Mass communication is mediated through such mass media channels as radio, television, cinema and press, video. This is essentially electronic media. Communication through mass media caters to the needs of the mass audience, for whom the messages are produced in mass, and distributed in mass, and are also consumed in mass. The distribution is done though these electronic mass media channels and even through traditional cultural media.

*2. **Functional:*** Communication can be labled as applied or theory related. Applied communication focuses on the practice of communication through various communication channels of mass media, interpersonal and folk channels. Applied communication has a social purpose, is action oriented and messages are communicated to create and implement practices.

Further, the different forms of applied communication include:

(a) Different types of messages through broadcast media of radio, T.V., video, cinema for informing, educating, and entertaining people.

(b) Journalism through print and broadcasting media.

(c) Communication through various communication

technologies such as telephone, fax, satellites, computers etc.

(d) Development communication through mass media and interpersonal communication channels to focus on development practices and programmes.

***3. Geographic:*** The geo related forms of communication focuses on intercultural communication between/among various ethnic groups; among various regions within a culture or ethnic groups. Intercultural communication is practised through mass media, interpersonal channels and folkways. Intercultural conceptualisations, theories and models are the foundation of intercultural communication. There is multinational efforts towards globalisation of today's world through international communication for political, economic, social, development and defence reasons through mass media and interpersonal forums. Such communication deliberations develop international communication theories and models.

**Major Functions**

Coming to communication functions, communication may be casual or phatic. When you say Hello how are you? It is a casual way of starting the conversation, it may just stop there or you may seek to set up further rapport and to seek further information. When it stops after Hello, how are you and the weather is good. It is phatic and it may not convey any meaning or information that is useful or true. But it is a good social lubricant. Phatic communication may be linear or interactive but the objective is not to seek information or reach at mutual understanding.

Communication can be directive or persuasive in order to stimulate thought, provoke questions, entertain, change and reinforce attitudes and behaviour. Therefore, the functions of communication could be informating, educating, motivating, and mobilising people. When communication functions are directive or persuasive; the objective is to seek or give information to educate and to motivate. Thus the communication is interactive, the experiences are shared and there is an effort to reach mutual understanding by sharing experiences, knowledge and ideas with others. When communication is functional; it aims at bringing three types of changes—creating awareness by disseminating information, attitudinal changes and changes in behaviour.

**Skill Development**

One must have skills to generate communication to create patterns of communication and to handle communication. The basic skills may be effective communication; evolving an effective communication strategy; and use of persuasive techniques and appeals, organising media forums. The first two we have already discussed.

Remarkably, in persuasion the emphasis is on attitude and behaviour change and not message quality. Some of the techniques used are:

(i) Role playing persuasive technique. This technique has the potential for changing attitude towards self.

(ii) Counter attitudinal advocacy. This persuasive technique requires that the intended persuadee be induced to publicly demonstrate a message which is at odds with his prior beliefs.

(iii) Negotiation—an interactive process to act the best transaction done. These techniques capitalise on the desire for involvement. These make people (persuadee) active participants in the influence process.

To pursue emotional appeals effectively is also a communication skill. Some of the appeals used effectively are: self-esteem, anxiety, fear, hostility, commitment, consistency. In organised forums of group discussions, meetings, lecture demonstrations, or other passive forums the communication skills are required in the use of projective and non-projective techniques.

**Organisation**

Basically, communication can be organised by communication rules, achieving communication competence and through developing communication networks. Communication events are not governed by laws of nature nor are they random and chance events. They are characterised by regularities and patterns. These patterns occur due to inherent tendencies, social norms or conventional rules. These patterns are specific to groups and communities. These are patterns of interaction. The patterns of communication i.e. how the content is presented is more important than the content of the communication per se. Such patterns of communication will be of interest in setting up co-evolutionary relationship between forms of communication and in ways of being human. These patterns of communication are not static but dynamic in nature and often repeated. But the limits of various social realities sometimes channel people into unwanted repeated patterns (U.R.Ps) of interaction.

Communication theories account for patterns for communicative behaviour in terms of social norms and conventional rules attributing motives, meanings and purposes to human actors involved in the episodes. These are RULES for explaining the communication behaviour or the operative behaviour model.

**Etiquettes**

Individuals may be modelled as a systems of Rules for meaning and action; the juxtaposition of two or more intrapersonal Rules system produces Interpersonal Rules system. The Interpersonal Rule system in term exerts Logical Force which control and constrain various lines of sequential actions. A human being is enmeshed in multiple social system with its own logic of meaning and action. For effective communication a person must coordinate and manage (organise) the logics of different systems. Logics must be coordinated by certain intrapersonal and interpersonal Rule systems. For effective communication, the communication contexts must be organised and coordinated.

These contexts are Physical contexts relating to geographic areas and regions; the Psychological contexts relating to the Psyche of the individual i.e. his/her motives, beliefs, attitudes behaviour and social contexts relating to social norms, community/society structure, national and international norms. Communication contexts organise the communication per se and for effective communication the multiple contexts must be organised and managed. The contexts are also governed by communication Rules. There are Constitutive Rules and Regulative Rules to process information. The Constitutive Rules describe one aspect of information processing i.e. assignment of meaning. The meaning is assigned according to the contexts. For example word, 'beautiful' is complementary if context is friends but it may be satrical insult if the context is an argument or an enemy. The Regulative Rules describe the process by which particular acts are felt appropriate. They are cognitive reorganisation of constitutive Rules. The Logical Force in the interpersonal Rule system is created by the combination of rules for meaning and action. There is Prefigurative Logical Force created by the cluster of variables. These variables link a particular act to elements in the rule structure that are defined as existing as prior to that act. These include range of acts and entailments of the act from the antecedent, episode, contact, life script, and archetype.

Pearce and Cronen (1980) argue that content refers to the referential cognitive processes by which individuals organise and interpret the world as it is ultimately perceived. Speech acts are the things one persons does to another by saying something. Speech acts are interpersonal exchange of meaning. There are referential and relational meanings. Contracts denote the propensity persons have to define relationships with others as things having particular attributes. Episodes are communicative routines which the participants view as distinct wholes, characterised by special rules of speech and non-verbal behaviour. Life-script refers to the repertoire of episodes that a person perceives as identified with him/herself i.e. the Self-concept. Archetypes (original patterns or Model) guides individuals not only in punctuating experience but common enough to make those punctuations communicable in spite of diversity of culture, situation and personality. Rules are descriptions on how persons process information. Constitutive and regulative rules are useful heuristics for describing the way they process information. Thus the persons are controlled or determined by the events around them.

When prefigurative force is high, people tend to act in ritualistic or habitual patterns. Practical Logical force is created by the cluster of variables which link a particular act to elements in the Rules structure that are defined as subsequent to that act and includes the range of acts and entailments from the act to the self, episode, contract, life script, and archetype. Practical logical force describes the persons as purposive agents, acting in service to their intentions. When practical force is weak in comparison to prefigurative force, persons are unable to achieve desired goals and persist in the act that entail undesired consequents. The concept of logical force describes the action chains that can be performed given the intermeshed rule of two or more persons.

In fact, the interpersonal rule system each person alternatively produces message according to his/her rules and the preceding messages. There is coherence, control and valence to coordinate these messages. Coherence is the extent to which persons make sense of the developing sequences of messages. Control is function of a person's perception of his/her ability to affect the ongoing sequence of conjoint behaviour in which they participate. Thus there are communication sequences which are coherent but perceived as out of individual's control such as learned helplessness; those that are coherent and controlled; or those which are incoherent and uncontrolled such as double bind. Those that are incoherent and controlled such as coordinated avoidance. Valence describes the person's evaluation of the emerging episode.

### Competence

Notably each one of us at one time or the other makes a judgement about the communication competence of someone—a reservation clerk, a police officer, a teacher, a telephone operator etc. It is easy to recognise communication incompetence. Incompetence in communication becomes obvious to us when we recognise violation of roles and rules that we believe should govern the interaction of the people.

Competence in communication is more difficult to define. As an intutive definition we may say what communication competence means is a person's ability to know how to say the right thing, to a right persons, in the right place at the right time. Competence is mutual understanding of the rule and roles of social interaction. Competence is related to behaviour and performance is the indication of the competence. A competence communicator knows how to analyse the interpersonal relationships and how various kinds of behaviour are going to affect that relationships. Communication competence implies judgement in evaluating relative effects—whether an act is appropriate or not, efficient or wasteful.

We should judge competence in specific contexts. The guidelines for evaluating communication competence can be appropriateness, efficiency, flexibility, and gratification. The primary element to successful adaptation in life is communication skills and the concerns are focused on communication competence. For the last few decades communication competence has been deliberated under various nomenclatures such as communication effectiveness, communication competence, functional communication, and interpersonal competence. Regardless of nomenclature the focus has been on success in communication. Powers and Lowry (1979) advocate Basic Communication Fidelity (BCF) as the basic concept of communication competence. BCF is the degree of congruence between the cognitions of two or more individuals following a communication event. Cognitions of source and receivers may be accurate/ appropriate or inaccurate/inappropriate on the basis of knowledge, standards and socio-cultural criteria. The 'social reality' agreed by members of the community play major role in traditional judgements of communication competence.

There are five generalisations:

1. The individuals must have access to signals and symbols within the receiver's framework of knowledge and associated denotative and connotative meanings. The greater is such access and knowledge, the greater is the potential for BCF.
2. A source must have the linguistic capabilities in order to arrange the signals and symbols comprehensible to the receiver. The greater is syntactic capability, the greater is the potential for BCF.
3. A source must have information processing skills including perceptual accuracy, decoding, encoding, neurological transmission, logic, intelligence and many more. The greater the information processing skills, the greater is the potential for BCF.
4. A source must have accurate awareness of the culture, society and the communication context in which the message will be transmitted. The greater the cultural, societal, contextual awareness, the greater is the potential for BCF.
5. A source must have sufficient physical and speech production capacities so that the receiver has minimal opportunities to develop cognitions congruent with the source. The greater the physical and speech production adequacy, the greater is the potential for BCF.

Pearce and Vernon (1980) suggest that communication

competence is the person's ability to move within and among the various systems he is cocreating and comanaging. Competence is relational, depending on both the characteristics of the person and the situation.

Further, competence is multidimensional. Most current concepts of communication competence establish a continuum between those who cannot and do not perform as expected (incompetent) and those who can and do perform as required (competent). Harris (1979) conceptualises the performance requirements as imposed by a system as variable and describe competence for examining relation of the individual and the system. The individual may be outside, inside, or beyond the system. Harris' Model of Communication Competence defines the individual's relationship to the system.

Minimally competent persons are incapable of moving in ways other than those prescribed by a given system (culture, society etc.); and optimally competent persons are capable of moving within or outside a given system at their choice; satisfactory competent person moves within the system when socially approved. Communication competence involves the interface between the individual and the system, particular individuals are probably minimally competent in some areas of social life, satisfactorily competent in others and optimally competent in still other areas. The development of the concept of communication competence is grounded in socio, political, economic development, and particularly the advent of modernity. Since individual communication competence is in relation to the characteristics of the social systems, the communication competence will vary with the requirements of the various systems.

## Communication Networks

Here it is noteworthy that social network theory assumes network in a social system for interpersonal interaction. Sociometery is the presentation of network data organised through sociogram and matrices. We get network data through sociometric questions WHO talks to WHOM. Social research in the past made sense of human behaviour by categorising individuals according to their individual and social characteristics. But currently we study and analyse human behaviour by mapping the communication structure of the individual in which he is a participant. Explanations of human behaviour are sought in the individual's communication links with other members of the system not in Linear Model but through Network Model.

The assumption is that information does flow horizontally, vertically, circular and in multiways between equals of shared interests. People communicate with each other, among themselves to influence and reinforce their attitudes and behaviour. The group pressure or group context reinforces the effects of selective perception and selective exposure as ultimately they must conform to group norms. The processural nature of communication flow suggests communication networking in a community or an organisation WHO is linked to WHOM in communication network depends on various network dimensions.

The communication network dimensions are connectedness, diversity, proximity, social and spatial link distance, and stability. The content dimensions of the communication network are topic related in two ways, i.e. the topic content determines the communication network. Thus there may be different communication networks for different discussion or information seeking topics. The

Communication Network determines the flow of content. The Content Network typologies are instrumental networks, friendship networks and personal and impersonal networks. Both social and spatial distances explain WHO is linked to WHOM. The principles of least effort and greatest reward also determine these Networks. A given individual may have different set of communication partners for each of the myriad topics. There is multiplexity i.e. the multiple contents flow through network links between individual. The multiple content can also flow through networks link between individuals. Multiplex links differ from uniplex links. The multiplexity can determine stability, connectedness, diversity, proximity and other network dimensions.

What makes a network link important is determined by the content flow of such links. How generalised network ties are across time. The generalisation is about the degree to which different content topics flow through the same network link and also the type of communication content that flows through these links. The content flowing through communication networks may affect the determinants of who interacts with whom. Research evidence is that information seeking links are more hetrophilious (on socio-economic status and other characteristics) than are friendships links (whom do you talks most). There is more effort and reward involved in the first. In a village farmers may seek information from more educated farmers with larger farms, so they link with hetrophilious links. Such hetrophilious links require more communication effort but getting information justifies the effort. Communication networks based on instrumental content are more stable than networks based on friendship. Both multiplex and stable links require greater effort.

As is obvious a communication network consists of interconnected individuals who are linked by patterned communication flows. The usual procedure of Communication Network analysis is: (1) identifying cliques within the system, (2) of identifying specialised communication roles such as liaisons, bridges, isolates in the communication structure and (3) measuring various indexes of communication structure such as low-high connectedness, diversity, proximity etc. for individuals, personal networks, cliques or systems. A link is a communication relationship between two units (usually individuals) in a system. Such links are usually measured by sociometric questions to indicate WHO communicates with WHOM. Other alternatives are observation of the communication behaviour in a system or other unobtrusive methods in which the observer is removed from the events being studied. Communication Network analysis is a method of research for identifying the communication structure in a system, in which relational data about communication flows are analysed using some type of interpersonal relationship as unit of analysis. It traces the interpersonal relationship as well as message flow in a system. It compares communication structure with the social structure of the system. This helps to determine how social structure is related with communication networks. The social structure is understood through the process of communication. Network patterns can be Dyads, Personal Networks, Cliques and Network Systems. Individuals are the units in all these networks. Dydic communication connects individuals who are some what hetrophilious.

Personal Networks consist of those individuals who are linked by patterned communication flows to a focal individual. In a radial personal network an individual interacts with a set of dydic partners who do not interact with each other. In an interlocking personal network, an individual interacts with a set of dydic partners who interact with one another. Individual integration is the degree to which members of an individual's personal network are linked to each other. So interlocking personal networks, are more integrating than radial networks. In personal network there can be direct links or indirect links resulting in first order personal network, second order personal network, or third order personal networks.

In a small group, a communication network may go through series of phases in its development. First, there is a relatively low level of interpersonal communication, as individuals do not know whom to talk to. Network links are mainly with others in a similar role, here Cliques emerges consisting of homophilious individuals.

At the second stage there is high rate of interaction as individuals begin to get acquainted. The cliques grow together to form a Connected Network as relatively weak ties bridge hetrophilious pairs of individuals. At the third stage, a high degree of stability occurs in the communication structure, and the rate of interaction levels off and decreases. This particular patterns of network change and stability may occur for larger systems depending on the other dynamic aspects of networks. In the process of network formation other dynamic aspects are: low connectedness, high connectedness followed by attrition of certain links so that more distinct cliques emerge in the communication structure.

How late entering members of a system gradually get interconnected into the network structure. How the size of cliques change overtime and how new cliques are formed within the same network. The network effects may culminate in strong and weak ties; and group and system performance.

A clique is a sub-system whose elements interact with each other relatively more frequently than with other members of the communication system. Average clique connectedness is the degree to which the average member of a clique is linked to other individual in the clique. Clique connectedness is inversely related to clique size. Systems (networks) consist of all the individuals and other units in a system. Such as in a village or organisation. The patterns of communication networks varies according to communication situation, varies from innovation to innovation, varies in different segments of society such as rural, urban and Rurban, and varies in males and females.

To conclude communication can be organised by communication rules, by achieving communication competence and through developing communication networks. Communication is a process whether linear or non-linear. In most elementary form the function of communication can be phatic or casual. It may mot convey any meaning or information but it is a good social lubricant.

Its function could be directive or persuasive for bringing three types of changes: creating awareness, by disseminating information, bringing attitudinal and behavioural changes and by educating and motivating people. The requisites for effective and successful communication are: Clearly defined objectives for the communication act. A knowledge of characteristics of the targeted audience.

Source credibility with the targeted audience. Source credibility must be backed with adequate information, knowledge, communication skills to disseminate information and the responsiveness of the audience to the messages. The presentation of message reinforced by repeated exposures over a period of time and through mixed channels of communication and presented in a conducive and appropriate communication environment.

## REFERENCES

Kincaid D. Lawrence 1979, *The Convergence Model of Communication* paper No. 18 East West Communication Center Hawaii.

Mead G.H. 1934, *Mind, Self and Society, from the Standpoint of Social Behaviourist,* Chicago, University of Chicago Press.

Narula Uma and W.B. Pearce 1986 *Development as Communication: A Perspective on India,* SIU Press Carbondale.

Narula Uma 1984, *Urban Communication Competence* paper presented at the ICA International Conference.

Pearce W.B. and Cronen V.E. 1980, *Communication, Action and Meaning,* New York, Praeger Press.

Pearce W.B. 1989, *Communication and the Human Condition*, SIU Press Carbondale.

Powers—and Lowry 1979, *Basic Communication Fidelity*.

Rogers E.M. and Svennings L. 1969, *Modernisation among Peasants the Impact of Communications,* New York, Holt Rinehart and Winston.

________and Shoemaker F.F. 1971, *Communication of Innovations: A Crosscultural Approach,* New York, Free Press.

________and Agarwala Rekha 1975, *Evaluation Research in Family Planning Communication,* UNESCO Technical Report, Paris, UNESCO.

________(Ed) *Communication and Development: Critical Perspective CA* Sage Publications.

Shimanoff Susan B. 1980, *Communication Rules: Theory and Research,* Sage Publications Beverley Hills.

Schramm Wilbur 1964, *Mass Communication and National Development,* Stanford, Stanford University Press.

________and Porter Williams (Eds) 1973 (revised 1982), *Men, Women and Media: Understanding Human Communication,* Honolulu, University of Hawaii Press.

________and Lerner D. (Eds) 1976, *Communication and Change: The Last Ten Years and the Next* Honolulu, University of Hawaii Press.

Singh Kusum Jitendra 1976, *Gandhi and Mao as Communicators: A Comparative Study of Practice and Theory*, unpublished dissertation, University of Philadelphia.

Singh Kusum Jitendra and Bertram Gross 1979, Challenges of Communication for Rural Reconstruction, *Media Asia* 6(1) 2-13.

Tolumin S. 1968, *Concepts and Explanation of Human Behaviour* In. T. Mischel (Ed) *Human Action,* Academic Press, New York.

Watzlawick Paul 1976 *How Real is Real,* New York Random House.

# 2

# The Nature of Mass Communication

> "Consider how hard it is to change yourself and you'll understand what little chance you have trying to change others."
>
> —*Arnold Glasow*

In the present chapter we intend to analyse the nature of mass communication. All salient aspects and issues are addressed suitably.

In fact, the mass media of communication includes social institutions that serve the society by compiling, writing, and distributing the news of the day. They take their character principally from our political and economic institutions, offering information and entertainment in the market to uncoerced buyers. Uncoerced means that the diverse mass public is able voluntarily to choose anew each day the media it will purchase and to which it will devote its time.

An effort has been made here to describe the market and its journalistic products, to observe their influence on other social institutions important to self-government, and to search ways in which the media may contribute more to the development of institutions that make up our civilization. The effort to adjust our agrarian political institutions to the present industrialized community specially affects journalism.

The mass media have the whole people as an audience and this fact makes their social importance apparent. Cold and hot wars waged with mass populations require mass media of communication and the maelstrom of propaganda places a premium upon accurate information usable in making stable decisions. Communication usually arises outside one's immediate group and cannot readily be tested for error. We are all of the information through mass media.

Bedeviled as we are by the pedlars of bias, it is difficult for a citizen to seek out and to evaluate information about any country, including his own, particularly if he gives attention to information that differs either from the official propaganda line or the line advanced by a powerful group. In theory, the mass media, are expected to maintain freedom of speech and discussion, but they are also under heavy pressure to bolster and sustain bias as if it were truth. In the strategy of communication, the masses in our society are deemed unsophisticated and easily exploited by demagogs, organised study of mass opinion processes has proved beneficial to friends and the enemies of democracy, and any distortion of information sabotages political processes based on reason and logic. Importantly "age of the masses" is the large scale of the political and economic instruments being used by the community.

Rivalry in trade, propaganda, and armaments is no longer between individuals and freely formed groups but between nations, and it is world-wide. The business enterprises developing the Tennessee, the Missouri, and the Nile are regional and official as well as private; labor activity is national and international in scope; merchants utilize a national and even international network of distribution, and they advertise over radio and television and through the networks of printed media reaching hundreds of millions of people.

Teams in soccer, baseball, football, and other sports have international followings, and are watched in action by television audiences as well as by those present in person. Desegregation is a regional issue politically important all over the world. When a leader speaks through print, film, or broadcast media, the effect on the masses, regardless of frontiers, is quickly visible; the impact excites those who wish access to these powerful agencies of influence and heightens the frustrations of those unable to achieve the results desired. Those who fail to persuade often blame the media rather than the message, and those who succeed often give the media more credit than they deserve.

In social interaction, words and acts draw their lively existence from one another. As with mind and body, it is difficult to separate them precisely and often impossible to determine the roots of words or actions. When students look at a social structure it is difficult to distinguish concrete forms from the words that describe them. Learning is illustrated by the familiar sight of a mother instructing her toddler to stay out of the street. When the child, his mother's warning ringing in his ears, steps into danger, only a good strong pull can bring him back to safety; further words are waste and futility. But the memory of the word coupled with the emotional gesture registers its meaning, becomes internalized as a barrier in the mind which the child cannot cross.

This is interpersonal communication, authoritative in

the sense that the mother and child are in a particularly intimate relation and the child knows, or soon will know, the love and power behind the command.

Basically, Social communication in a democracy takes place between individuals or groups and the element of authority is not present or not dominant. When the communication is mediated through print or broadcasting, the relation between the communicators is relatively indirect and voluntary, the frame of reference is less intimate, and the messages are more generalized. The interposition of mechanical media has changed communication in the same way that the orator is changed when, moved from the platform to the stage, he merges with the collective personality of the players.

He still uses rhetoric, logic, and persuasion, but his words now are not necessarily his own, and his effect on the audience is dependent on the course of the action in the play, upon characters supporting and opposing him, and on the brooding omnipresence of the playwright. Most students of communication seem to assume that the media can be separated from society and studied as if they had a virtually independent existence.

Such an assumption creates a static and unreal field of observation. Thus the history of the Reformation and the Renaissance can be told as a history of writers and printers making use of Gutenberg's new movable types. Modern war can be seen as a struggle between rival teams of propagandists vying for control of the minds of men while cannon and bomb blast away indecisively. A political campaign can be pictured more as Rosenman (the speechwriter), Russell Davenport (the political idealist), or Batten, Barton, Durstine, and Osborn (the mass communicators), than as Roosevelt, Willkie, or Eisenhower.

Such versions of events may be nearer to reality than the formal, full-length portraits of conventional political history. But more often they distort conventional political history by snapping the shutter on one instant of life and displaying the snapshot as typical of the whole. Separation is a device for directing attention to one part of social structure while neglecting its organic unity. Society is the basic organization of mutually dependent family, kinship, and kindred-interest groups that provides for exchange of labor.

Social organization has so grown in complexity that it is everywhere more visible than the individuals caught up in it; we speak of the age of the masses and think of work and ideas as being the product of groups rather than of individuals. Communication has advanced from its interpersonal orientation in the family and small groups to the point where it also takes place on a national and international scale. The typesetting, printing, and broadcasting machines of the communications art have ended the isolation and separation of communities within particular societies.

Cultural uniformity in such communities tends toward homogeneity, and society must deal with this sameness, as it did with cultural diversity, in terms of its impact on personal and group interests, upon social goals both sought after and in being. The influence of social institutions. Mass-communications media are social institutions, the product of a social demand, even though they appear to be self-propagating. The human personality is shaped decisively by the family and by interaction with significant other persons in the community; particularly in infancy and youth, but all through life, the individual is sufficiently plastic that role, attitude, skill, and behavior alike can and do change.

The individual has an influential original nature of his own; together, the original nature and the social environment constitute the matrix of personality, a matrix assumed not as a completed shape but as being built up gradually of units of experience. The acceptance by the individual of any one unit of experience leads to more formative interaction. When the individual becomes mature, that is, relatively habituated in the way he ingests new information and processes it, he can see the separateness of particular aspects of his personality and, if he has sufficient insight and will, can bring about further modifications and integrations.

But for most persons the opportunity for self-analysis and for change is quite limited. Personality appears much more substantial than the will can easily alter. The individual, through his attitudes and beliefs, and particularly through his susceptibility to fear, is sensitive to the import of mass communication — though not so sensitive, perhaps, as in an intimate frame of reference. But when the opportunity for rational action comes, he responds to his knowledge. Significant others may channel and interpret information for him and persuade him to act in concert with them. If countervailing factors are present, however, he retains his freedom of choice.

Practically, the pressure of communicated demand or need helps create institutional forms whose purpose is to do the work of the group. Thus economic institutions are constructed to provide food and physical facilities for life and political institutions take up the roles of rulemaker and arbiter. There are formal definitions of such institutions.

"Any well systematized and effective social psychic mechanisms that satisfy basic, or what appear at the time to be basic needs, that enhance the ability of social groups to maintain themselves and persist, that control the individuals and groups within a society, whose demands are generally thought to be right and that have the power of enforcing themselves, are institutions.

The mass-communications industries are institutions with functions located centrally in the network of social relationships, ranking very high in any arrangement of institutions according to social importance. The family, the institution which has grown up around the sex drive and the attendant task of rearing children, might occupy the first category in such an arrangement. The institutions of agriculture and business, satisfying the need for food, are on the same level as the family. Government is next, and language and writing, out of which the mass communications have grown, are either a part of government, as in totalitarian countries, or on a level of their own, in countries where society and government have separate identities and separable institutions.

The labels "authoritarian" and "democratic" are loosely applied to governments. The function of the press in either system is to provide communication that establishes the reality of social institutions and facilitates control of them. In the authoritarian systems, journalists are under the discipline of the ruling group and willingly help shape and condition individuals according to plan. In systems that try to reconcile diverse groups and their different concepts of social function, the press is the agency by which the constituent groups in society become aware of their differences and are brought to accept intercourse based on the principle of toleration. When contending groups recognize the importance of public communication they want to use it for selfish ends, but if they are frustrated in this desire they then demand communication that is accurate and fair to all. Government is in the same central position. Where the party system tolerates controversy it outlaws violence and lets the franchise depend upon peaceful activity. Like other social institutions, the political grew out of man's need to conventionalize differences and make possible orderly political action.

Political history shows how difficult it is to confine parties to orderly procedures free of violence and how closely political stability follows the fluctuations of economic well being. What we describe as stable government is the rather direct product of an economic situation in which individuals and groups eschew violent forays because their basis needs are met, or because the system promises fulfillment of needs in return for reasonable and non-violent effort.

Struggle for self-improvement must be conventionalized. Where authoritarian parties rule, the communicators, journalists, intellectuals of whatever kind, must accept the task of obtaining acceptance of the decisions of the ruling group. In much of the West the journalist is a collaborator with parties, groups, governments — a partisan and teacher of controversial ideas. He also, in some cases, aspires to be a reporter, a vehicle for the objective transfer of information, somewhat above the battle, equally important to all contestants because he serves all equally well, an instrument indispensable to modern civilization.

The idea that the individual has basic rights, as well as duties, was articulated in ancient and medieval society as in modern. The state's claim on the people's loyalties is predicated on the benefits they get in return for performing duties assigned them by the state. The differences among political systems are qualitative; they concern the kind of relation between the individual and the state of which he is a citizen. This theory originates in the experience of the people, in the interaction of the preferences and actions of the constituent groups in society. The role of the intellectual theorists is to provide options from which the people choose. Once the choice is made, the literary theorists describe and interpret it, law gives it stability, and education attempts to perpetuate it.

Here it is worthy to note that the The contribution to political liberty made by Anglo-Saxon tribal and village life was an understanding relationship between the citizen and the officials. Whether the leaders were elected, chosen, or accepted by the group in some other way, the continuity and dignity of tribal custom and common law was understood by both leader and led and there was opportunity for the people to utilize the prestige of law in opposition to the prestige of leadership, although the relative political strength of the individuals concerned may at times have put little restraint on the executive power.

But the fact that law and leadership were recognized as community products and that they ran separate if parallel courses in the life of the community, provided the fundamental ethic from which all claims of men against the power of government developed. In the English-speaking world political and religious controversy, beginning with the conflict between English common law and William the Conqueror's concept of national landlordism, developed a system of politics and jurisprudence lodging sovereignty, or ultimate power, in the people. There are bright figures in the controversy: Sir Edward Coke, who upheld the common law as the law of right and reason in the face of royal prerogative; John Milton, whose plea for unlicensed printing was directed at a parliamentary dictatorship from the intellectual ground of a Greek temple of justice, the Areopagitica; John Wilkes, whose activities as politician and editor helped open Parliament to public reporting and gave greater security to the system of party government; Richard Carlisle and his family, whose unequal struggle with authority established the opportunity to sell and distribute printed matter as equal in importance to the right to print without prior censorship, and by thousands of writers, printers, and readers who stood in their time before authority, in the tradition if not with the same effect as did Coke before James I, to assert the supremacy of law. When James said to Coke that he, too, as well as common-law judges, had reason, the Lord Chief Justice replied that it was true that God had anointed the king with "excellent science, and great endowments of nature," but the king was "not learned in the laws of his realm of England, and causes which concern the life, or inheritance, or goods, or fortunes of his subjects are not to be decided by natural reason but by the artificial reason and judgment of law, which law is an art which requires long study and experience before a man can attain to a cognizance of it." James replied that it was treasonable to suggest that he should be under the law; the course of his action stemming from that attitude led to civil war, to the Revolution of 1688 and the supremacy of the views expressed by Coke.

**Communication in a Democracy**

Coke is a figure symbolic of the primacy of law interpreted by professional judges. Milton represents the ideal community in which controversial discussion proceeding freely among all who wish to speak was counted upon to facilitate a reasonable consensus. This model community, free to discuss and to decide, was secure in the faith that truth would win out over error in public debate. It was projected in the *Areopagitica, a speech of Mr. John Milton for the Liberty of Unlicensed Printing, to the Parliament of England,* published November 25, 1644. The book was practical in intent, for a complaint against Milton was on file in the House for a previous breach of the licensing ordinance, and Milton wished not only to escape punishment but to publish still more. In particular he wanted to agitate for reform of the laws of marriage and divorce, partly because under the influence of her Royalist family, his young wife was then living apart from him and he, a vigorous adherent of the Parliamentary camp, despaired of a reconciliation.

He knew that the Stationers' Company, which had a government printing monopoly, was under the influence of the clergy and would not license a publication so heretical. But the *Areopagitica* was addressed to broader and more general problems than Milton's domestic troubles. The country was in a civil war brought on by controversy over the role and power of bishops. There were at least three distinct parties with positions on this issue well defined and Milton was advising his own party, then in control of Parliament, that it could safely entrust its cause to unlicensed and uncensored public discussion. "Let Truth and error grapple," he assured the parliamentarians, "who ever knew Truth to be put to flight in a free and open encounter?"

Since Milton's statement of principle was uttered in a controversy having religious content, it is appropriate to turn to the lives of two great religious figures for illustration of how this theory worked out in practice. Siddhartha

Gautama, founder of the Buddhist faith, was the son of a king and designated heir to the throne. After a period as deputy civil administrator he found himself opposed by a faction headed by Prince Devadatta.

Frustrated by this opposition and in disenchantment Siddhartha went into a nearby wilderness where, living as an ascetic, he worked out a philosophy and set himself up as a teacher. He had great success but old political enemies plotted against him. They left the body of a young prostitute beside his hut and spread a rumor that he was her murderer. His disciples, ready in the human pattern to believe the worst, turned away from him indignantly.

Rejected, deprived of mission, Siddhartha returned to his home city. Here he found that his enemies had preceded him and that they were sedulously spreading their false report. Moreover, to intensify the public's reaction to their great lie, they placed the body of the girl on a litter and carried it through the streets. To the litter a banner was attached naming Siddhartha as the slayer. Afterward, the body and the banner were transferred to a funeral pyre to await gathering of the village residents. The people of Siddhartha's home city reacted in the same way as the colony of former disciples. As the people turned against him, Siddhartha was caught up in a raging encounter of truth and error; it seemed certain that error would prevail because he could not think of a way to communicate his case as forcefully and effectively as his enemies had purveyed the lie.

The imminent victory of error through the use of an ugly, dark smear would make it impossible to gather another group around him to teach his hard-won philosophy. In addition, he faced loss of patrimony, exile, and rejection by the community he had sought to serve. There was only one counter-action he could take, to mount the funeral pyre and shout out the truth to the unbelieving crowd. As he summoned desperate courage for this act, he was rescued by the timely intervention of authority in the person of his father. Sizing up the situation at once, the father turned on Siddhartha's enemies and obtained the testimony of an informer and a confession from the principal. Truth was again in the field, backed by superior force. The chief conspirator was convicted and set off on a procession behind the same litter. The ugly banner was corrected to absolve Siddhartha and to identify the guilty. There is a parallel demonstration of the Miltonic theory in the life of Jesus of Nazareth, whose career illustrates how important a part friendly authority played in the experience of Siddhartha. On the day when Jesus carried the cross through Jerusalem, the political power and prestige necessary for his rescue was not in friendly hands. Recognizing this, Jesus occupied his final hours by setting in motion plans for continuation of the struggle the climax of which was a ritual of resignation and acceptance. The struggle was to continue beyond the grave. Truth as a function of political control. The experience of these two spiritual leaders makes clear an aspect of the theory Milton understood acutely but which he neglected to make clear.

Truth victorious is not passive; it is always at war, hot or cold, and those who wish to see truth succeed tend to come into action with all the weapons at their command. They can hope to win only if the centers of authority are in friendly hands. Effective truth is not mere communication, but the control of the state and of the machinery of enforcement of decisions. When the followers of Jesus organized and instituted teaching missions in an essentially hostile environment, they needed conventions that placed great charismatic value on tolerance and protection of the heretical individual. In need also of agents and agencies of communication, the Christian protagonists used those they found—students, leaders, itinerant evangelists, housewives, all who showed interest. Where these agents of communication found it possible to go freely and openly about their work, they made friends and eventually challenged the special interest groups opposed to them. The threat of cunning and violent opposition always hung over them, as it did over Siddhartha, and when a community rebelled under the impact of the new ideas authority was called upon to decide between the antagonists; once force was used the opportunity for further discussion addressed to the issue was at an end. Others might later pick up and go forward with a similar discussion, but violence, as communication, is impossible to reverse.

In fact, the press is an institution that learns from experience, just as individuals do, and learning tends to be passed by one generation of managers to the next. Since its experience during its identity with political parties was of formative significance, we should take a longer look at what happened.

Towns in the new states came to have three, four, and five newspapers, along with business allies engaged in land speculation; but this kind of diversity was hardly as enlightening as pure theory would require us to believe. A prejudiced journal read by a prejudiced mind is a far cry from the dream of many informative media in the market place of thought, for even if the people read, as Jefferson wanted them to do, how shall they understand? Jefferson's view of the blindly partisan press was that it canceled out its usefulness. This experiment was wanting for the world to demonstrate the falsehood of the pretext that freedom of the press was incompatible with orderly government. We have never, therefore, even contradicted the thousands of calumnies so industriously propagated against myself. But the fact being once established, that the press is impotent when it abandons itself to falsehood, we leave to others to restore it to strength, by recalling it within the pale of truth. Within that it is a noble institution, equally the friend of science and of civil liberty.

The journeyman journalist and editor made the diversified party press possible. A close look at one such polemicist might help to show why party newspapers fell out of fashion and demonstrate that it was a miserable press produced by unhappy men not averse to finding greater security and satisfaction in different employment. Jefferson looked upon himself as a teacher of political ideology; his interest in the press stemmed in part from his need for assistance in spreading his ideas as far as possible. For this reason he supported the *National Gazette,* edited by Philip Freneau; the help he gave another journalist, James Thomas Callender, was similarly motivated. Callender was a penurious English political refugee resident in the United States, trying to make a living by serving whatever patron he could find. After passage of the alien and sedition laws he left Philadelphia for Richmond, thinking he might be personally more secure there while continuing work in his libelous art.

He contributed to newspapers and wrote a political pamphlet smearing President Adams for which he was punished under federal law by a two-hundred-dollar fine and a jail term. In jail or out, Callender had never earned enough to cover his living expenses, keeping up a stream of begging letters to his political patrons. Jefferson, a frequent contributor, helped again while the journalist was in jail. After Jefferson became president, Callender demanded a political appointment and when he did not get it he turned ferociously on his patron. His libels of Jefferson, when reprinted, resulted in the case against Croswell in which Hamilton contributed his services as attorney.

But Callender's lot did not improve with the switch in allegiance; his family was dependent upon what he could wheedle and beg. Besides, he was by now a proved political renegade, considered unreliable by both parties. The future, at best, promised only more of the same. Such journalists and such journalism were only as secure as the political fortunes of their allies. These activities made up the competitive age of diversity and tarnished the bright hope for the tournament of reason held out by Milton. The principal social gain was that the frustrating of Callender's tribe served to turn journalists away from careers in the art of political vilification and lead them to search out a more satisfactory base for a living.

One other major dispute with political overtones helped round out the political theory of freedom of the press in the nineteenth century. A federal judge in St. Louis, sitting in a dispute over public lands, was criticized by a lawyer living outside the jurisdiction of the court. The judge, in the usual hearing without a jury, punished the lawyer for contempt and was, himself, then impeached in an effort to remove him from office. The effort failed, but the Congress and most of the states then made such use of the contempt power unlawful. The state courts gave up the authority grudgingly and took it back in a series of decisions only to lose it again in an opinion by the United States Supreme Court in 1941.

The press has been vulnerable historically to the use

of the contempt power and this is a critical area in the dynamics of government and press relations. By 1941 the United States courts had undertaken to guarantee freedom of the press as "among the fundamental personal rights and `liberties' protected by the due process clause of the Fourteenth Amendment from impairment by the States." This left the press in a strong position so long as the federal government was more liberal than the states in its attitude toward freedom; if the situation were to be reversed, the press would be back to the conditions of 1798 when Jefferson took up its cause and saved it from repressive federal controls. The one indispensable tenet in the theory of communication that flows from this series of events is that the people must believe they have an irrevocable right to freedom of speech and press; and they must be willing to remove, by decisive political action, restraints upon their enjoyment of the right.

Milton's model of the society of open communication was incorporated in 1791, as part of the Bill of Rights, into our Constitution. The original Constitution itself had assured freedom for business, for it contained something of the spirit of Adam Smith's *Wealth of Nations,* published the year the American Revolution began. Smith applied the Miltonic ideal to relations between government and business, arguing that society would be better off if production of goods geared to bar subsistence gave way to wider opportunity to pursue individual economic aims. He advised free competition in goods as Milton had urged free trade in ideas. He trusted men as reasonable and ethical beings capable of learning from personal and social experience; he felt them inclined toward sympathetic consideration for others, and able to adjust their activities accordingly. This was the self-righting process of ethical society; it was the process that Smith, like Milton, counted upon to monitor competitive practices. The statement of the theory of freedom of information on the political and legal levels must, therefore, be supplemented by an examination of the economic level. The theory in the hands of businessmen is equally important, for the modern shape of journalism stems from the work of these men. The majority of editors and publishers were content with neither the poverty nor the political misery of the Thomas Callenders and sought a greater degree of economic security.

The natural and historic association of journalism with politics could hardly be abandoned at once, but the general growth of business, and the equally natural and historic association of the press with advertising offered a way to improvement. Business and politics were hardly separable or distinguishable, but the ideal of political and economic independence grew inside the press.

### *The Discovery of Mass Readership*

The first and second American dailies were business ventures hopefully designed to cater to the needs of business growing in the new climate of freedom. The second one succeeded where the first one failed; but it was not in an appeal to advertisers, but to readers, that the daily paper first found promise of new vigor and independence. The New York *Sun,* a penny paper published by a job printer who had little interest in politics, and less in Wall Street, was the first to take hold of the general public. This paper was sold copy by copy on the streets directly to readers instead of by annual subscription payable in advance. In a year it had twice as much circulation as the higher-priced newspapers oriented to business and politics. Its focus was largely on plain people and the problems common to humanity, police-court cases, and the varied human tableaux of passion and violence. It had a feeling for adventure and escape that was rudimentary in form but appealing to the unsophisticated human heart.

The *Sun* proved a true pioneer, the creation of an entrepreneur whose insight into the mass mind was fundamentally sound. Its success accounts for the first element in the new economic theory of the press: Go after wide readership. Mass-periodical circulation was built by assuming that most men live on the level of the senses and that to them the urges, needs, and frustrations of the self are the things of most importance. When a businessman undertakes a venture involving trial, error, and risk — as Day and his imitators did — he follows essentially the procedures scientists describe as empirical and pragmatic. The important difference is that the scientist publishes a record of his experience and invites other students to improve on his procedures and broaden the predictive value of his results. The businessman does not. If the results of entrepreneurial effort are successful, if a satisfactory profit is produced, the information as to method, results, and the probable predictive value of the data is treated as secret and held in reserve for future struggles against competitors, present and potential. If the venture is unsuccessful, the entrepreneur sometimes has to reveal his data before a referee in bankruptcy; even so, only a few businessmen will attempt to evaluate unsuccessful experience and to make use of it in future ventures. Because much of the information upon which entrepreneurs base their strategy is circulated by word of mouth, and speed with which explanation of both success and failure is transmitted is slow. Moreover, the fate of nearly all business ventures is decided by the march of events rather than by the conditions at the time the original decision to invest was made.

The march of events from 1830 was favorable to the

mass-circulation paper but Day's contemporaries soon saturated the market with their product. Technology produced the semi-automatic machines necessary for a large growth in circulation, with papers delivered to readers on the day of publication, and for a large increase in the daily average number of pages. Another entrepreneur, the merchant, needed publicity to guide to him a tide of customers gradually rising with increases in population and disposable income. Thirty-five penny papers started in New York alone in the 1830's and only two survived. But in spite of difficulties, the idea of the mass-circulation paper spread around the world. James Gordon Bennett founded the *New York Herald* five years after the *Sun.* He took Day's human interest formula and developed it on a regional, national, and international level, gradually stimulating a public appetite for news as a viable commodity for which part of each day's pay had to be allocated. Merchants of many classes began to ask him for large advertising spaces and he was able, after a mechanical breakthrough in stereotyping and press design in 1854, to develop the *Herald* into the most profitable newspaper of the moment — a purveyor of news and bold reports of the excitement that human beings find in their common vicissitudes. The *Sun* and the *Herald* were edited by Democrats and this fact made the field look attractive to Horace Greeley, a journalist and political writer allied with the Whig party. He established the New York *Tribune* in 1841 as a penny paper with opinions.

He developed the editorial page so successfully that he is rightly credited as the inspiration of the leadership-page tradition in the American newspaper, a tradition of despair as well as glory, for while a journal may lead one willing segment of its readers who crowd close on its heels, it must suffer the disapproval of another segment, often larger than the first, that does not like either the ideas or the politics with which they are associated.

The financial success of the *Tribune* excited the interest of the men who established the New York *Times,* Henry J. Raymond, a former editor on the *Tribune* staff, and George Jones, a banker and former employee in Greeley's counting room. Greeley's style of thinking and writing, and the sensationalism of the *Sun* and *Herald,* left Raymond and Jones a market for content based on wide coverage of news, moderation in editorial opinion, and objectivity in place of sensationalism. The competitive struggle following establishment of the *Sun* emphasized circulation growth. The daily newspaper press that emerged from the competition for circulation was oriented more to business, including its own economic welfare, than to politics.

An eye witness was frank Munsey, who assigned himself the role of broker and liquidator after mushroom overexpansion had put several of the most respected firms into difficulty. He wrote in 1898 that the development of journalism as a business was influenced most by James Gordon Bennett with his *Herald* and that the transition to the stage of big business was due chiefly to the impact of Joseph Pulitzer and his daily and Sunday *World.* Edith Merwin Barstow says that the pressure the sensational newspapers put on the conservative publishers forced changes in content through heavy competition for mass circulation. She writes: "Leading the confused and bewildered conservative publishers were the yellow journals. Frenzied in their power, their unlimited fields for exploitation, and their determination to dominate competition, the converts of the Yellow Kid created and fed the hysteria that demanded more news, shocking news, improbable news, news with scareheads and banners and appropriate pictures.... Risk to invested capital multiplied with mounting costs of newsprint, presses, tools, talent, wire and feature services. Conservatism and caution were imposed on the press by hard facts, and puzzled publishers looking for guidance beheld success in terms so contradictory that confusion was worse confounded; the public granting life to newspapers was unfathomable, unpredictable, imperious, and inflexible."

Helen MacGill Hughes adds further detail: because of the coverage of sensational human interest news by Bennett and others, she says, the circulation of the daily papers grew by 187 per cent between 1830 and 1840 while population was growing only 32 per cent. Bennett's popularity was "as natural as that of a talkative sheriff or coroner," Mrs. Hughes says, for in coverage of crime and murder stories he shared all the gossipy details with the public. His skill and boldness brought down upon him the wrath of the conservative newspapers of New York, who cloaked their envy in moral indignation. Even the archbishop of New York was moved upon one occasion to threaten Bennett with excommunication because of stories in the *Herald*.

The content of Bennett's paper might offend his competitors, as the relative size of their circulations declined in comparison with his, but though the elite groups may have objected, the masses did not. Instead, their purchases of the *Herald* raised its circulation to record heights. The human-interest story soon had even a wider range than Bennett gave it. With Dana and the *Sun* it was gentler, often with a tinkle of laughter or a twinge of pathos in it; with Robert Bonner of the New York *Sunday Ledger,* it had the big names of statesmen, ministers, and literary lights he obtained as contributors, and in the strong, simple appeal of love, struggle, and mystery in his fiction. With others, as for example the editor of the *Police Gazette,* the deviation was in the direction of crime and violence.

The success of Joseph Pulitzer encouraged imitators who say only the *World's* sensational material, not its effort at a balanced presentation of news and opinion. These imitators used extreme display of news of scandal, crime, and violence and won circulation in New York City despite the popularity of the *World, Herald,* and *Sun.* Proprietors throughout the country sought quick increases in circulation. "Eventually most newspapers recovered from the disease, but modern journalism has exhibited some of the effects of the curse of yellow journalism ever since."

Munsey lets us see inside the counting rooms of some of the publications competing with leaders like Hearst and Pulitzer. From the owner's point of view, he said, the "most heartbreaking publication is the one which is almost breaking even. But it either should be enlarged in plant and facilities so as to become profitable or it should be discontinued at once." He estimated that a million dollars a year was being lost in New York from such publications' almost breaking even. The price at which these papers were sold to the public had to be the "lowest possible to discourage competition and encourage consumption," he said, for while readers are not slow to recognize extra value and to follow a new leader, they "won't follow anything but the successful journal." It makes no difference to them if the maker of shoes they buy is near bankruptcy, "but they won't follow the near-bankrupt journal." These economic facts accounted for the effort to build the human-interest type of content, for it was far more popular with the readers than more serious material. And it retains its popularity.

Twenty years later, with competition still intense in spite of the closing of a number of newspapers, a new series of deliberate efforts was made to push human interest in the news well beyond the limits of good taste, and oftentimes beyond the legal limits of decency as well. This was the period of jazz-age journalism which began in earnest after World War I and was checked only by the great depression. One of the most successful of the practitioners of this brutal art was Emile Gauvreau, trained on the conservative Hartford *Courant,* but coming to prominence as editor of Bernarr Macfadden's *Morning Graphic,* known in the trade as the pornographic, and of Hearst's *Mirror.* Gauvreau said that in retrospect the yellow journalism of the early twentieth century was simply an exploration by the papers of the full possibilities of the vast new mass audience.

Not so jazz-age journalism. It was, said Gauvreau, an offshoot from the parent stem, and was dedicated to the fullest extent to the primitive instincts of mankind. Its object was to attract attention at any cost, and the most intimate details of life, in a period noted for its excesses, appeared in the sensational press along with smashing displays of crime news and an occasional crusade for better conditions in local government.

"The news-stands of the country at the time were swamped with sensational magazines, a large number of them of the art and sex variety." Gauvreau claimed it was to this audience that he appealed with his paper. *True Story* magazine had two million circulation and the sex magazines of other publishers had a combined circulation of nearly fifty-six million. Gauvreau estimated that publications of this category had at least two hundred million annual readers.

The sensational *Graphic* and *Mirror* attained large mass circulations but could not succeed financially because advertisers withheld their patronage. The great depression followed close upon the experiment testing the profitability of sensational content. Like the jazz age, the depression was a symptom of problems men did not understand and could not discuss in wholly meaningful terms. Economic assumptions accepted on a wide scale had brought industrialization and great prosperity to urban areas.

All at once the economic plan broke down. Why? Failing to find answers, governments in various parts of the world floundered and were replaced, but the same journalists struggled with the new problems in an effort to explain them to the people. Conscious of inadequacy, they introduced college-trained men whose numbers steadily increased until the old type of journalist-craftsman was no more. As new economic assumptions based on the Welfare State drove out the chaos of the depression, journalism turned seriously toward the new mass society and the age of big government to report incident and trend as meaningfully and as accurately as it could. But the depression adversely affected the press by hastening the process of concentration of ownership. The newspaper count in the country dropped from 11,689 weeklies, semi-weeklies, and tri-weeklies in 1930 to 10,182 in 1960. Raymond B. Nixon reports that daily papers declined from 1,942 in 1930 to 1,763 in 1960. This left only sixty or so cities with competing daily newspapers and although radio and television established alternative channels of communication and undoubtedly reached a mass audience, their content was prevailingly entertaining rather than informational. The theoretical basis of the democratic self-righting process seemed impaired if not destroyed, and the New Deal years in which the press found itself in a politically weak position intensified doubts, aroused by consolidation, that a basis for diversity existed any longer.

All of these things — Greeley's great contribution as an editor using the exciting tools of reason and as the producer of a newspaper with cosmopolitan interests, the high news standards of the *New York Times,* the gentle humor of Dana, the composographs and lurid paragraphs of Emile Gauvreau — made up the reputation of the press, and as with all reputations the bad stuck more firmly than the rest. The twentieth-century press had tried out several ideas on the market and had a theory it thought would work. Together with the political theory of diversity, these findings constitute today's practical theory of the press system:

1. The press system provides an opportunity for openness and diversity of communication in support of the political ideology. A diverse community is made up of innumerable special interests pressing their claims upon the general society. For a time, newspapers of general circulation were published by and for particular interests of one kind or another, but these publications proved poor competitors with others that provided information and entertainment as well as — or in lieu of — propaganda.
2. The form of association and of government developed by the community gives first priority to diversity of political and religious ideas and second priority to corporate unity. The system of thought assumes that institutions for cooperation and government can be constructed under conventions that will force compromises among competitors for political power.
3. The competition for circulation had one particular goal—sale of space to advertisers. This brought problems of content and standards which, on their own account, are still to be resolved.

4. Owners of newspapers discovered that human-interest stories—news about the joys and tragedies of the human struggle—were marketable to a wider audience than was serious information. They used this discovery to build mass circulations. They also found, because many newspapers carrying it went bankrupt, that the market for human interest, like that for information, was limited. Simultaneously, some of them learned to develop other devices for competition — crusading and muckraking, special correspondence from news centers at home and abroad, news enterprise and promotions, editorial pages, special features of several kinds.

In the foregoing discussion, various issues pertaining to nature of mass communication are suitably addressed. Understanding of these is essential for every professional in the field. Various theoretical approaches to communication are discussed in the next chapter.

# 3

# Theoretical Approaches to Communication

> "Two things, well considered, would prevent many quarrels; first, to have it well ascertained whether we are not disputing about terms rather than things and, second, to examine whether that on which we differ is worth contending about."
>
> —*Charles C. Colton*

As we all know, modern communication theory springs from a variety of intellectual fountains: psychology, sociology, anthropology, philosophy, political science, psychiatry, and even electrical engineering—as well as the professional communication areas such as speech, English, journalism, radio and television, and cinema. There is, in fact, no single communication theory, just as there is no single psychological theory. Rather, we find a flow of research and theorising, bound by a concern with symbolic behaviour.

A scientific theory, in its purest form, is a distillation of the complex data of life into its crystal essence. They theory is a set of statements, including some lawlike generalisations. The statements must be deductively related. And some of the statements should be empirically testable. Unfortunately, in the social sciences today, we do not have many fully formalised, well-articulated scientific theories to gladden the heart of a rigorous philosopher of science. We do have some partially formalised theories and numerous probes which may eventually escalate into full-fledged scientific theories.

In communication, especially, we have been blessed with a plethora of "models." In the philosophy of science, a model has a somewhat ambiguous standing. Some equate model with theory. Others see 'model" as a broad umbrella, covering everything from visualised ignorance to tolerably well-formalised scientific theories.

**Communication Models**

For the most part, today's popular communication models are first steps toward theory—initial cuts into a complex and dynamic process. The typical model pinpoints key elements—crucial variables that must be considered if we are to understand communication. The model always selects; it cannot consider all of the elements that might be encompassed. Further, a model abstracts; it moves up from the concrete until it finds an inclusive term like "source," which blankets the teacher, the actor, the reporter, etc.

Having sorted out the crucial components of the communication process, the model usually specifies organisation; that is, how the elements are inter-related. Finally, particularly in the predictive models, we find propositions about the process itself. Beyond laying out the elements and their structure, the model explicates the dynamics; it details the operations. It predicts: If this variable changes from this state to that state, then that variable will change also.

***Who Says...?***

There centuries before the Christian era, Aristotle

outlined a primitive communication model when he said that rhetoric had three major components;

(a) the speaker,

(b) the subject, and

(c) the person addressed.

He went on to specify that the third, the audience, was most important in shaping the message.

In the last century, political scientist Harold Lasswell elaborated on Aristotle's sparse verbal model. To adequately describe a communication system, Lasswell concluded, one must ask:

*Who*

Says *What*

In which *Channel*

To *Whom*

With What *Effect?*

Notably, model provided the launch pad for Lasswell's probes into political communication, propaganda, and political symbolism—some of the pioneering communication research in social science.

***Signals and Noise***

Lasswell's work in the 1930's was followed by theorising from quite another sector in the 1940's. Claude Shannon's wartime work culminated in "information theory," and Warren Weaver, writing in *The Mathematical Theory of Communication,* provided a visual model of Shannon's communication system.

The Shannon-Weaver model comprises five key components:

1. an information source, which produces a message;
2. a transmitter, which transforms the message into a signal suitable for transmission;
3. a channel, which carries signals from transmitter to receiver;
4. the receiver, which reconstructs the signals into a message; and
5. the destination, the final consumer of the message.

The model introduces a final—and novel—component: the noise source. Shannon recognised that communication always takes place in the face of "noise," interference, and the natural tendency toward deterioration. A key problem for Shannon's theory was: How to you most efficiently overcome noise? How much redundancy is necessary so that the receiver can successfully reconstruct a message from signals decimated by noise? Weaver saw three levels of communication problems: Level A, the technical problem; how accurately can the symbols of communication be transmitted? Level B, the semantic problem; how precisely do the transmitted symbols convey the desired meaning? Level C, the effectiveness problem; how effectively does the received meaning affect conduct in the desired way? For Weaver, Shannon's theory was clearly directed at Level A, with strong implications for Level B and C. Others have humanised Shannon's admittedly mechanical model. The words "encoder" and "decoder" have replaced "transmitter" and "receiver." Boxes for "semantic noise" have been added to the box for "channel noise". But perhaps more important, the Shannon-Weaver visual model provided an impetus for the visual modelling of the 1950's and 1960's. The guts of Shannon's theory are not captured, however, in Weaver's visual representation. The visual model isolates components and diagrams their organisation. But the process of this system is detailed in Shannon's mathematical formulas.

He demonstrated a unique way to measure "information," and armed with this measurement he sliced through a host of traditional problems involving coding, channel capacities, and the design of communication systems. While Shannon's original focus was on electrical telecommunication, the theory proved to have wide applicability and diffused rapidly into such diverse fields as biology, optics, sociology and psychology.

***Attitude and Communication***

While Shannon was generating information theory, psychologist Carl Hovland was immersed in attitude research for the armed services. His findings propelled him into a large-scale postwar study of communication and persuasion. To guide his research, Hovland adopted a classificatory model. Laid next to the Shannon-Weaver model, the Hovland scheme highlights the proliferation of variables needed to predict effects in human communication. Hovland was primarily interested in predicting attitude change, although for him this included opinion, perception, affect, and action change. He noted that in any communication situation, observable communication stimuli could be grouped into characteristics of the content, the communicator, the media, and the situation. He suggested that individuals might differ in their predispositions toward communication stimuli.

Some, for instance, might be influenced by communicator-bound factors while others might be affected more by media-bound factors. And among media characteristics, some might prefer visual stimuli while others might prefer aural cues. The observable communication stimuli, interacting with the predispositional factors, lead to the internal mediating processes of attention, comprehension, and acceptance.

### *Perception and Communication*

Whereas Hovland's communication model focuses on the attitudinal output, George Gerbner designed a model which gives emphasis to the perceptual input. Stated verbally, Gerbner's model says:

1. Someone
2. perceivers an event (or statement)
3. and reacts
4. in a situation
5. and through some means
6. to make available materials
7. in some form
8. and context
9. conveying content
10. with some consequences.

It is noteworthy that central to the communication process, for Gerbner, is the message. This is the social act which makes possible inferences about events not directly observed. Gerbner is therefore interested first in the perceptual dimension—the communicators viewpoint, his relationship to the world he sees. Next, he is interested in the "means and control dimension"—the relationship between the communicator and the statements he makes. Finally, he is concerned with the correspondence between event and statement—the truth dimension. The statement, of course, becomes an event in the perceptual field of another communicator.

### *S-M-C-R Model*

One of the most widely used communication models is the S-M-C-R model, developed by David Berlo. It is simple and versatile, yet it subsumes an enormous background of behavioural science theory and research. S-M-C-R stand for the four key components—source, message, channel, receiver.

*1. Source.* To predict the source's effectiveness, we will want to know about (a) his communication skills, (b) his attitudes, (c) his knowledge, (d) his social and cultural context. First, is he literate? Does he have the skill to create pictures? to manipulate language? Next, what are his attitudes toward his receiver? toward his subject? toward himself? Third, what is his knowledge level? Does he know his subject matter? his receiver? himself? Finally, what are the roles and norms that shape his communication behaviour? Does he speak as a member of a political group? a religious group? a professional group? Does he start from certain cultural assumptions, such as the Indian values of individualism and progress? Or does he come from a culture where progress is rare, where kinship is stronger than self?

2. *Message:* A message has content—the what's-it-about? And this content appears in some code—English or French, picture or word. The source selects contents and codes and weaves them into his treatment, his style, an his tone. Content, code, and treatment can be analysed on various levels. At each level, elements can be isolated. These elements are organised into structures, which, in turn, become elements at the next highest level of analysis. The written English code has letters for elements; these elements combine into words. At the next highest level, these words become elements which, in turn, combine into sentences.

*3. Channel.* The message reaches the receiver through some channel. It may be "natural"; one of the sense modalities, seeing, hearing, touching, smelling, tasting. And it may be an "artificial" channel, such as television, radio, newspaper, telephone. One implication of the model is that more than one channel may be used at once. The selection and patterning of these channels may affect the total communication outcome.

*4. Receiver.* Like the source, the receiver has communication skills, attitudes, knowledge, and a socio-cultural context. Each may contribute to his capacity as a receiver. In addition, for each category, we may wish to examine the relationship between source and receiver. If, for instance, both have positive attitudes toward the topic under discussion, communication may be facilitated. Or, if the source falsely assumes the receiver has common knowledge, the stage is set for a communication breakdown.

In recent presentations of the model, Berlo includes the important concept—feedback. The source's message to the receiver typically elicits some behaviour, and some of these become available as messages which can be fed back to the source. On the basis of this information, the source may modify his successive messages. In a dynamic communication situation, of course, two individuals may shift rapidly back and forth between source and receiver roles. In fact, in conversation, an individual usually plays both roles at once, sending verbal messages through the air while receiving visual messages about the hearer's reactions.

### *Mass Media*

Bruce Westley and Malcolm MacLean, Jr. elaborated on the roles communicators can play. Their model is especially helpful in analysing the complex media, where teams of communicators mold the message. A four-stage model, the Westley-MacLean design grows out of an earlier model by Newcomb in which Person A transmits something about an Object X to Person B.

*Stage 1.* Westley and MacLean first show Receiver B selecting from the objects of orientation—labeled $X_1$ through $X_{infinity}$—in his sensory field. Not all objects are selected, for example, $X_4$. The selections are based, in part, on B's needs and problems. The objects reach the receiver in abstracted form, represented by the small x's-$x_1$, $x_2$, $x_3$. And some or all may come via more than one sense; for example $x_3$ and $x_3m$.

*Stage II.* Westley and MacLean next introduce Communicator A, who selects and abstracts X's, transmitting them as Message X' to Receiver B. Communicator A has an intent; he not only wishes to transmit X's, he wants to structure the receiver's perceptions. He would like to influence B. The objects of orientation may or may not be in B's direct sensory field. For example, information about $X_1$ is transmitted directly; *i.e.*, $x_{1b}$, and indirectly, $x_1$, through A. Finally, Receiver B provides feedback, $f_{ba}$, to Communicator A. He may or may not intend to modify A's behaviour with this feedback.

*Stage III.* As an alternative type of communicator, Mr. C is introduced. Communicator C selects and abstracts objects of orientation which definitely are not in the normal sensory field of Receiver B. In the Westley-MacLean model, Communicator C is seen as "non-purposive." He extends Receiver B's environment, but he does not intend to influence B. The selections C makes for Receiver B are based in part on the feedback, $f_{BC}$ from B.

*Stage IV.* In its final complex form, the model simulates the situation that might be found in the mass media or the classroom. Receiver B gets messages, $x''$, from Communicator C, a reporter or a teacher. C gets information from three sources: He has messages, x', from purposeful Communicator A; he may have additional direct information, such as $x_{3c}$, on topics Mr. A discusses; and he may incorporate information, such as $x_4$, on topics not transmitted by Mr. A. Receiver B provides feedback, $f_{BC}$ and $f_{BA}$ to C and A. C similarly provides feedback, $f_{cA}$, to Mr. A.

### *Other Models*

Remarkably, the 1950's brought a flurry of communication models. Bettinghaus reviewed thirteen of them, including the sociologically oriented Riley and Riley model. More recently, Miller has discussed models, including Kelman's model of opinion change, and a model emphasising non-verbal communication.

In the 1960's, the era of general model building seemed to wane. Scholars turned attention to special problems within the communication process. Mathematical modelling became more important, and computer simulation began in earnest. Attempts were made, for instance, to simulate interpersonal communication, the diffusion of information through a population, an audience's choice of television programmes, and legislators' communication before a vote.

(a) The communication process is complex;

(b) The modeler typically isolates key components, such as the source, message, channel, and receiver;

(c) Depending on his interests, the modeler isolates the characteristics, or variables, important to each component—for example, the source's attitudes and knowledge;

(d) The modeler may try to specify the possible states and each variable—e.g., high or low knowledge for the source, positive or negative attitudes for the receiver;

(e) He moves finally toward stating relationships—e.g., high source knowledge leads to high receiver attitude.

## MESSAGE SYSTEMS

Message systems can be defined within or between; that is (a) within the system of components, such as code, content and treatment, which make up a message, or even among sets of messages, as in an audio-visual presentation; and (b) between the message and the source, or between the message and receiver, or between the message and the referents encoded.

***Semiotic***

An early attempt to logically organise the study of message systems can be found in Charles Morris' semiotic, the science of signs. As formulated by Morris, semiotic has three domains:

(a) syntactics, the study of sign-to-sign relationships;

(b) semantics, covering sign-to-referent relationships; and

(c) pragmatics, roughly sign-to-interpreter relationships.

Basically, the relationship between a sign and its referent exists, of course, in the mind of interpreter. Thus, we really have three overlapping spheres: Pragmatics includes semantics and syntactics; semantics includes syntactics. For Morris, each area of semiotic can be subclassified as pure, descriptive, or applied. Pure semiotic develops a meta-language to talk about signs, while descriptive semiotic analyses actual signs, and applied semiotic uses knowledge about signs to accomplish various purposes. Communication theorists have been interested in each area. They have tried to develop more precise vocabularies for talking about codes. They have been interested, for instance, in content analysis, with actual signs. And they have examined the effective use of signs for a variety of goals.

We will broach the subject of signs by first discussing codes and code systems. What is necessary for a code to exist? First, we need some stimulation which is above the sensory threshold of occur recendor.

Finally, we need a set of agreements that certain variations in the patterned stimuli will refer to objects and events outside the code. We may decide that three dots and a dash will stand for the letter "V." Or, Secret Agent Triple-Naught may arrange a code: "When I draw the blind, you close in."

Miller has noted that humans seem able to handle around seven elements at a time. When elements proliferate, we begin to "chunk,," or re-code. A complex code system, like human language, is enormously complex and efficient. It handles tremendous amounts of information and operates at several levels at once. While language has received the most attention, we are coming to realise that man uses many code systems, frequently without ever consciously learning the code.

### *Code Systems*

Each of the fundamental motor acts, such as uttering or scratching, can produce patterned stimuli, usable as a code system. Martin Krampen has organised a set of motor acts showing the code systems arising out of each act. Each has a basic code element, such s the phoneme, and these elements combine into structures, such as the morpheme, which become elements at the next highest level of analysis.

Linguistics, now more than a century old, is most advanced. Kinesic, now in its third decade, has made substantial gains, particularly through the research of Ray Birdwhistell. An area like pictics is relatively new, and some of the code systems are virtually unexplored.

In addition to the ten suggested by Krampen, Edward Hall argues that time and space can be patterned into code systems. He calls the study of space "proxemics." Both can be organised into isolates, sets, and patterns, comparable to the phonemes, morphemes, and syntax of spoken language. Krampen's analysis permits us to re-examine communication systems in terms of the codes used. For instance, the lable "audio-visual communication" suggests a channel orientation.

### *Multiple Codes: Interband Congruence*

Given multiple codes, or even one complex code, it becomes possible to create messages which are simultaneously redundant—or conflicting. Osgood and Sebeok speak of communication "bands," such as the linguistic band, the kinesic band, and the situational-manipulational band. Between-band organisation can provide information which agrees, disagrees, or is essentially independent. Ruesch and Kees discuss "meta-communication"—communication about communication. In other words, in each message there is information about some referent; there is also information about the message and how it should be interpreted. The source may encode cues which tell the receiver: "This is important." "Listen especially to this." "This is kidding; don't take it seriously." In multi-code communiques, of course, meta-communication may flow in a separate code. Illustrates the pairing of a simple linguistic morpheme—"now"—with three different face pictomorphs. The faces lead us to reinterpret the "now." For Face I, it seems to be: "Now—Oh Boy!" For Face II: "I mean do it *now!*" Face III is, itself, a complex message. It contains the simile of Face I, a cue of happiness, plus the frowning brows of Face II, a menacing cue of anger. Used simultaneously in one face, the cues no longer seem simply happy or simply angry.

In the three illustrations, the between-band organisation is essentially complementary. Different information is provided by each code. It is like a smiling face saying, "I'm thinking of Liz." Without the smile, you wouldn't know how he feels about Liz. But without the statement, you wouldn't know what is making him smile. In addition to complementary organisation, bands can be redundant. A smiling face says, "I'm happy." Or the bands can be in conflict, providing different and countermanding information. A smiling face says: "You rascal!" The various alternatives mean that a great deal of uncertainty can be absorbed—or stimulated. Hence, the amount of information transmitted can vary greatly.

### *Codes and Capacity*

In information theory, Shannon provided some major break-throughs on problems of coding and channel capacities. To get at least some flavour of Shannon's thinking, we might note that for Shannon a "bit" of information is that which reduces uncertainty by one-half. We can see that choosing between two equally probable alternatives, I and

II, involves one bit of information. Choosing between four equally probable alternatives—A, B, C, or D—involves two bits. Choosing between eight alternative involves three steps, or three bits or information. Uncertainty increases as the number of alternatives increase. And uncertainty increases if alternatives are equally probable. (A 50-50 situation is more uncertain than a situation where the chances are 90-10). Building on his definition of information, Shannon was able to calculate the capacity of communication channels, compute the information and relative redundancy within a message, and provide some surprising theorems about how best to encode information for a noisy channel.

He noted, for instance, that as a code, written English is about 50 per cent redundant. You could knock out every other letter and, with enough patience, a receiver could reconstruct your message. Taylor, has used this idea to develop "cloze" procedure, a test for readability. He blanks out every fifth word and the receiver's ability to correctly replace the missing word is an index of reading case.

### *Code-Referent: Iconicity*

The relationship between a code element and its referent is usually arbitrary. We say "horse." The French say "cheval." Spaniards say "caballo." Each is equally adequate—as long as the users of the code agree. But for some codes, such as pictures, the relationship between element and referent is "natural" rather than arbitrary. This is known as the iconicity dimension. Morris suggests that a sign by called iconic if it has some of the properties of the thing it represents. The power of the iconic sign, for Morris, lay in the receiver's ability to respond directly to the properties presented. Ruesch and Kees speak of iconicity in terms of analogic and digital codification. The analogic symbol is similar, in proportions or relations, to the idea, event, or thing encoded.

Digital codes are meanwhile discrete and deal with arbitrary step intervals.

They give numbers and the phonetic alphabets as prime examples. For them, the coding system have sharply different potentials, especially in coding aspects of time and space. The psychologist James Gibson talks of iconicity in terms of "degrees of fidelity." The full fidelity "surrogate by projection" presents to the eye the same sheaves of light that the original would present. A "surrogate by convention" does not. It stands for something in the same way a license plate "stands for" the car it was assigned to. Edgar Dale's "cone of experience" deals with the coding of information along an iconicity dimension. Writers like A. Korzybski, Wendell Johnson, and S.I. Hayakawa have similarly wrestled with the implications of coding objects and events into abstract symbols.

### *Code-Receiver: Sign, Signal & Symbol*

Generally, people receive a vast number of stimuli every day. We might say that man's environment "communicates" to him constantly. The sun "communicates" its warmth. The car "communicates" its noise, its odour. But usually we find it convenient to distinguish between those stimuli that speak for themselves, and those that have communication values: *i.e.,* mean something beyond themselves. Morris calls these communication stimuli "signs," and he distinguishes two kinds: signals and symbols. A signal stands for something else in the way smoke stands for fire. It is a stimulus which heralds some other event. Meanwhile, a symbol is more explicitly encoded, and stands in place of its referent. The word "fire," or a picture of a fire, stands in place of the actual flames.

### *Code Preference: Visualisers and Verbalisers*

Berkeley, a British scholar once became interested in

the creative processes of great men. He asked some of his well-known peers how they visualised things; for instance, a year. To his amazement, he found that some of his friends thought him quite mad; they had none of the visualising facility he had. He concluded that there must be "visualisers" and "verbalisers." Continual anecdotal evidence supports Berkeley's notion, but this dimension of encoding and decoding remains somewhat cloudy. Yale psychologist Leonard Doob spent much energy exploring the reported "photographic memories" of primitive African tribes. Enthused at first, Doob now feels this "eidetic" ability is a will-o-the-wisp which is to elusive for firm observation. Earlier, Victor Lowenfeld developed his theory of the "haptics" and the "optics". The former are touch-oriented, while the latter are visualises. He operationalised the types in terms of the pictures they drew, and he suggested that they had different needs in art education. Perhaps some of the firmest evidence on the issue comes, from analyses of intelligence tests. Louis Guttman, for instance, has made a facet analysis of intelligence which indicates two major dimensions.

The first is an inductive versus a deductive type of ability; in other words, the capacity to generalise to a rule from a set of examples, as opposed to being able to apply a rule. The second dimension deals with the code used: verbal, numerical, or pictorial-geometric. Some individuals, of course, are adept with all three codes. Others may be high in one, but low in the remaining codes. In another line of research, psychologist Jeffery Shapiro recently developed a test which appears to distinguish linguistically oriented individuals from non-linguistic types. The test was developed out of face pictomorphs. The face is paired with a caption, and an individual's response indicates whether he is giving more weight to the words or to the picture.

While great individual differences probably exist, some writers have argued that a particular culture may shape verbalisers as opposed to visualisers or haptics. It's been argued, for instance, that the Puritan tradition was very word-oriented. Pictures were considered evil, there was a systematic attempt, in clothing and furnishing, to provide minimal sensory stimulation.

### *The Medium as a Message*

Marshall McLuhan argues: "The medium is the message." At one level, this suggests that the content of the message is less important than the way in which it's received. McLuhan, a student of Harold A. Innis, takes a long historical view. Innis used to take a crabby delight in pointing out that words often turned out to be less important than the materials they were written on. Papyrus, for instance, revolutionised the social control of ancient Egypt, putting the priests in command. In modern time, McLuhan argues that radio permitted Adolf Hitler to take command. And, according to McLuhan, we understand all too little the implications of the electronic revolution going on around us. We have moved, he says, from the pre-Gutenberg period, to the point where man is again returning to a tribal village, this time on a world scale.

McLuhan sees technological development as an extension of man. A shovel extends man's arm. A bow and-arrow extends his reach in another way. Clothing extends his skin. An auto extends his legs. Similarly, new communication technology extends man. The telephone extends his voice and hearing. Writing does the same; but it also extends his memory. With computes, McLuhan feels that we may be extending man's central nervous system, changing the way he can sense and think about his universe.

McLuhan suggests that the print media encourage man to think in a linear, segmented fashion, whereas the electronic media surround man in a mosaic. He further argues that some media, like movies, are "hot," while other media, like television are "cool": A hot medium extends one sense in "high definition," which, he says, means being well filled with data. He even sees countries as being "hot" and "cold": The backward countries are cool; the developed countries are hot. In Luhan's writings, the theme "classroom without walls" reappears as he argues that this generation needs to study the "grammar of its media" as well its content.

**Receiver Systems**

Receiver systems, like message systems, can be defined within or between: (a) the psychological, symbolic process within a receiver, and (b) the sociological, interaction processes among sets of receivers.

***Perception: Structure and Function***

Perception is an enormously complex human process. And it is an important process to anyone interested in multiple-channel communication. We will point here to merely two sets of factors which have dichotomised perceptual phenomena: structural and functional factors.

The structure of the stimuli and the perceptual equipment of the receiver lead to certain impressions. Some stimuli are perceived as figure, distinct from surrounding ground. This, of course, suggests, patterned stimuli, the basic requirement for a code. The Gestaltists in particular have pointed to those characteristics of the stimuli (proximity, common movement, closure) which lead to the preception of a coherent form.

Meanwhile, social psychologists have been interested in the impact of emotions, moods, needs, and desires on perceptual processes. A hungry man sees food in an ambiguous stimulus. A valued object, like a coin, is judged larger than it is. So is a threatening object. These and other findings have led psychologists to the conclusion that the internal states of the individual play a surprisingly important role in what and how the receiver will perceive.

***Arousal***

A stimulus, once past the perceptual threshold, speeds through the central nervous system to the cortex of the brain for interpretation. On its way, however, it feeds information to the reticular arousal system, a column of nerve cells in the lower brain. This system, it now appears, plays a crucial role in activating the individual, in attention, in alertness. It may, in fact, be the heart of all emotions; what are usually called emotional states may be periods of high arousal overlain with cognitions which are pleasant, fearful, sad, and so on.

Berlyne relates the arousal system to attention, which, in turn, can be related to learning. Of interest to the communicator, Berlyne has spelled out some of the stimulus conditions which lead to arousal. He notes first that moderate rates of arousal may be most efficient. With extreme arousal, the individual goes into shock; with too little arousal, he becomes inattentive. Berlyne sees the following as determinants of attention;

(a) high-intensity stimuli;

(b) colour;

(c) indicating stimuli—a pointing finger, a verbal, "Now heir this";

(d) novelty;

(e) surprisingness;

(f) complexity, uncertainty, and incongruity;

(g) conflict.

The last four categories are especially important in arousal. Novelty, for instance, depends not only on the unusualness of the stimulus, but also on how long it has been since a similar stimulus was received. In general, the opportunity for novelty, surprisingness, complexity, and conflict would seem to multiply with multiple codes and multi-bands.

### *Meaning*

The symbolic process is at the heart of man's ability to communicate, and communication theorists have been vitally concerned with the problem of meaning. Under what conditions and why, should some pattern of stimulation come to "mean" some other pattern of stimulation?

The early mentalistic view, as represented by Ogden and Richards, said simply that something becomes a sign of some referent if it gives rise to the idea or thought of that referent. Behavioural psychologists, of course, wanted to know why this was. In the tradition of Pavlovian conditioning, the substitution view was suggested: A sign, through conditioning, comes to elicit the same reactions in the individual as the real referent would. Obviously, however, the sign does not elicit all of the same reactions. The word "fire" does not evoke the same responses as the actual flames. This led to the dispositional view, articulated by Charles Morris. In essence, this view says: A pattern of stimulation becomes a sign if it produces in the individual a "disposition" to make any of the responses previously elicited by the actual referent. Psychologists like Charles Osgood have since tried to boil the ambiguity out of the term "disposition."

### *Representational-Dispositional*

As an explanation of the meaning process, Osgood has suggested the representational mediation hypothesis. Wired-in reflexes, such as the knee-jerk response to a tap on the pattella, lock reactions unfailingly to certain stimuli. In symbolic behaviour, however, a stimulus sets off a pattern of small, internal responses, which though learning, become the internal stimuli for other, perhaps over, responses. The response chain can in effect be unlinked if other internal stimuli impinge.

From the Osgood model, we can see that the receiver may be responding at several levels simultaneously. With complex messages, particularly with several codes and multiple sensory channels, the response process can become extremely complex. In certain learning tasks of course, we may be trying to teach the receiver to respond to a complex set of stimuli simultaneously and on several levels.

Remarkably, major varieties of meaning have been classified: denotative, connotative, and structural. Words (or for that matter, pictures) denote objects, events, and conditions. The word "mother" points to a woman who has a specific kinship relationship to another human; the word can be used to denote a particular person. But "mother" also has strong connotative associations. People are likely to feel it's a strong, active, positive word. Finally, we know that the word "mother" is a certain type of word. It is used in a certain way in sentences. We know that with 'mother" we use "is" and not "are". Words, in short, have structural significance; they play roles in the larger organisation.

Some words, of course, are strongly denotative, *Chair, ball, house would* be examples. Other terms—such as *beauty, democracy, dishonour*—tend to be connotative. And many words—*but, of, from*—are largely structural.

What has been said of the verbal code applies also, of course, to the pictorial code. A caricature can denote a politician. It can also stimulate connotations; the politician can be made to look like a hero or a bum. Pictures, too, have structural rules—within a single picture, and between pictures, as in a comic strip or a motion picture. The pictorial element which is large and overlapping other elements is seen in the foreground. The film shot that dissolves is seen as being in a different time or place than the succeeding shot.

***Semantic Space***

In one of the most extensive empirical studies of meaning ever made. Osgood and his associates found three main dimensions of what they called "semantic space": the evaluative, potency, and activity factors. The evaluative dimension is define by polar adjectives such as "good" and "bad". Potency is defined by such scales as strong-weak and hard-soft. The activity dimension is anchored by scales like active-passive and excitable-calm. To measure meaning, Osgood uses the "semantic differential." With this instrument, an individual can indicate his meaning for any concept. In the concepts "mother" and "coward" represented in semantic space. "Mother" is seen as good, strong, and active. "Coward" is seen as bad, weak, and passive. Using the semantic differential and the concept of semantic space, Osgood and his associates have also developed the "principle of congruity." Given an individual's meaning for two concepts, Osgood can predict what meaning will arise when the concepts are paired. This has been especially useful where the concepts are a communicator and his subject.

### *Cognitive Systems*

Osgood's principle of congruity parallels the thinking of other theorists; in a cognitive system there will be a strain toward equilibrium of consistency. Newcomb observed this equilibrium phenomenon in his A-B-X model. If source A is liked by Receiver B and Source A makes favourable comments about some object X. Receiver B is under pressure to think favourable of X. Fritz Heider and Leon Festinger elaborated their own consistence theories. Festinger called his a "theory of cognitive dissonance. He noted that any decision is likely to cause dissonance; a choice of one alternative means giving up the advantages of the other alternative. He predicted that in a dissonant condition, an individual might increase his information-seeking. Festinger found, for instance, that new car buyers may increase reading ads for their own brand of car—after buying.

Milton Rokeach explored "belief congruence" within his theory of the open and closed mind. He theorised that an individual's belief system might be visualised as three concentric circles. The inner circle of primitive beliefs include the individual's unquestioned beliefs about himself and his universe; for instance, what his name is. Authority beliefs specify the authority figures the individual follows, and peripheral beliefs include all the other beliefs held by the individual. Of interest to the communicator, Rokeach suggested that some belief systems are "closed" and some are" open". The closed system places strong reliance on authority; may have low tolerance for dissonance; does not discriminate well among disbelief systems (beliefs other than its own) and; finally, may practice" isolation," holding conflicting beliefs apart so they are never examined together.

In communication, the closed individual may have trouble discriminating meta-communication from content; information about the source will strongly influence response to the message.

Rokeach developed a scale to index one aspect of a receiver's cognitive system. Osgood's semantic differential provides another way to map a receiver's system and changes in that system over time. Other psychologists, like George Kelly, have innovated additional ways to map what Kelly called an individual's "personal construct system." A continuing theoretic problem, however, is the process of maping the receiver's symbolic system and measuring changes that occur during communication.

The S-M-C-R model points to the social-cultural context, and a broad array of research underscores its importance. We might ask first if it makes any difference how communicators are linked together. In a series of experiments, Bavelas, Leavitt, and others organisd communicators into various patterns, such as the circle, the chain, the Y, and the wheel.

In the circle, communicator A could only pass messages to *B* and *E*. *B.* could communicate with *A* and *C,* and so on around the circle. In the wheel, *C* held the central spot and could communicate with everyone else; they, however, could only communicate with *C.* The various nets were then given simple problems to solve. The different linkages affected accuracy, total activity, the emergence of a leader, and the satisfaction of group members. In general, the circle and the wheel were most different, with the chain and the Y falling between. The circle tended to be active, leaderless, unorganised, often inaccurate, and yet was enjoyed most by its members. In the wheel, *C* tended to emerge as leader and he enjoyed his role, but other members were distinctly less satisfied. The wheel tended to be stable, well organised, less active, and less erratic than the other networks.

A man in his role of employer may talk one way to an employee. The same man, in his role as father, may talk in quite a different way to his son; he may even use different language. Communication theorists have long been intrigued with the various roles that can be played in the communication process, such as the "gate-keeper" role or the "opinion-leader" role. Other theorists have elaborated role theory and have examined the consequences of "role conflict" and "role communication". In small-group research, Robert Bales suggested that distinct communication roles may emerge. He hypothesised that as a group works on a problem, a task leader is likely to emerge; an individual who actively asks questions, clarifies objectives, and gives answers. But as a group moves toward task-solution, internal frictions are likely to arise.

Unless socio-emotional needs are met, the group may fly apart. So another role emerges: the socio-emotional leader who gives praise, releases tension, and soothes ruffled feathers. Sometimes one individual plays both roles, but in the family, for instance, the father often plays the task-leadership role, while the mother assumes socio-emotional leadership.

If a group is asked to judge an ambiguous stimulus, norms will develop that are quite firm—though they may be totally inaccurate. These norms, once rolling, exert enormous pressure on group members. If, for instance, a naive member hears everyone in the group report an incorrect observation, he is under tremendous pressure to deny his own senses and report what everyone else did.

If a group member deviates from group norms, communication to that member will typically increase. Finally, however, communication to the deviant will be cut off. In effect, he's ejected from the group. When a group is under attack, of course, norms become more rigid and members have less freedom to deviate.

Norms may vary in the amount of deviation allowed, and in the sanctions levied. Jay Jackson for instance, used the classroom as an example. The group, probably led by the teacher, can express approval, illustrated by the scale +3 to -3. The norms could concern any classroom behaviour, but Jackson used as an example the number of times a student is expected to communicate during a class period.

### *Diffusion Through a System*

Notably, we can observe the diffusion of a message, a new idea, or an innovation through a population, and learn much about the communication process. Rumour studies, for instance, focus on what happens to a message as it passes from communicator to communicator. Typically, the message is subjected to a process of levelling, sharpening, and assimilation. Some elements drop out. This gives the remaining elements increased importance, and frequently they are elaborated even further. In addition, the message may be assimilated to the beliefs, attitudes, and expectations of the communicators. The message becomes systematically distorted until it "makes sense". Mass media theorists have long been concerned with the diffusion that takes place between media and mass audiences. At first, a widely held assumption favoured a "one-step" flow; the media were presumed to have a direct and uniform effect on the public. Later research indicated that individuals varied widely in their response to the media. Their exposure patterns, their reference groups, their individual beliefs and experiences substantially modified the impact of the media.

A "two-step flow" seemed a better hypothesis. The mass media fed key opinion-leaders, who in turn informed their followers. This hypothesis was sounder than the concept of a one-step flow, but recent research indicates that this hypothesis, too, is an oversimplification. Depending on the topic, and depending on a variety of receiver characteristics, the mass media are used in a complex variety of ways. Everett Rogers hypothesised that in the adoption of an innovation, mass media may be particularly important at the early, "awareness" stage. At the later evaluation and trial stages, interpersonal communication may be more significant. Rogers categorised receivers into innovators, early adopters, early majority, late majority, and laggards. The characteristics and the interaction patterns of each category have been studied across a broad range of innovations, and across several cultures.

As with any system, we may wish to raise questions about the viability and success of the system itself. Does it, for instance, have cohesion? Have the communicators developed, or maintained, positive attitudes toward each other? Are there other constraints or rewards which will keep them interacting? Is the system stable? or is it likely to be reorganised? Is the system productive? Is it effective? If this is a teaching situation and the decoder's recall is the most important output, is that the variable that is indeed changing? How efficient is the system? Is the decoder's recall changing with a minimum expenditure of the encoder's resources and energy?

Decoder outputs include immediate message responses: attention, comprehension, acceptance, recall, and use.

Outputs also include longer-range changes in skills, beliefs, and so on. The decoder responses may give rise to feedback which can be picked up by the encoder. This helps him to shape further messages.

Some of the factors which impinge upon the decoder's reception and interaction of the message include perceptual factors, arousal, levels of meaning, attitudes, beliefs, and finally, interacting with these, roles an norms. A similar set of factors pattern the communication behaviour of the encoder as well.

Many facets of the communication process have been omitted in this discussion. We have skimmed lightly over problems that are significant for the theorist and the practising communicator. We have, however, reviewed some of the major currents of contemporary theory and perhaps, pointed a few routes for further exploration.

**Communication and its Role in Instruction**

The typical model of school instruction appears to embody communication as an obvious and prominent component. This is the model in which a teacher stands at the front of a room containing thirty students and conducts various kinds of verbal communication with them. The teacher may tell things to students, orally, or write them on a chalkboard; he may elicit communications from the students in the form of oral or written answers to questions; or he may invite students to formulate more extensive communications to other members of the class in the form of oral or written reports. When conceived in this manner, instruction may seem to be simply a kind of directed and structured conversation. It is tempting, even, to consider the possibility that instruction is simply equivalent to communication.

There is much interest nowadays in computer-assisted instruction. Here, too, however, those who are engaged in serious research with this new tool recognise that the conception of a computer as a means of storing and locating information to be presented constitutes only the simplest part of what must be accomplished (cf. Suppes, 1966). Programmes and routines of various degrees of complexity must be designed to engage the human learner in activities that require him to accomplish many kinds of codings and transformations of the materials displayed. And these transformations, in turn, create needs for even greater varieties of units of information to be communicated. It seems clear, therefore, that one cannot simply equate communication with the process of instruction. Communication in its broadest sense of an event involving apprehension of a situation may be said to be an inevitable part of instruction, but by no means the whole. Thorndike (cf. Joncich, 196l, p. 74) pointed out that a common error of the scholar, inexperienced in teaching, was to expect students to known that they were told. "Telling," he said, "is not teaching."

The purpose of the process of instruction is to bring about a change in the capabilities (knowledges, skills, attitudes, and other dispositions) of the human learner. At some particular point in time, it many be determined that the student is not capable of executing some class of performances, let us say, adding sets of two-digit numbers. Activities that are called instruction are then undertaken with the aim of making it possible for the student to change his starting capabilities, including his inability to add two-digit numbers, to a new set of capabilities that includes this latter one, as indicated by his performance when given a sample of such numbers to add. The change that takes place as a result of the instruction is referred to as learning. Although he may frequently play other roles, the student is functioning as a *learner* while in the instruction situation. When he learns, his capabilities at time $x$ are changed to a new set of capabilities at time $x+1$.

To conceive of learning as a change in human capabilities is a first step in understanding the process of instruction. Such a view accomplishes two major clarifications. First, it puts the emphasis for instruction where it must be—one the student. However elaborate or complicated the process of instruction may turn out to be, or may be designed to be, its outcomes must be referenced to the changes that take place in the student. Whether instruction involves a teacher, a textbook, a class, a motion picture, a television set, or whatever, its ultimate function is to bring about a change in the student. As will be seen latter, the kinds of communications that form a part of instruction must also be judged in relation to changes in the capabilities of students. A second kind of elucidation arising from this view of learning is that the outcome of instruction pertains to its emphasis on a inferred internal state, or capability. Sometimes, it is said that learning is a change in "student responses" or "student performance."

While this manner of referring to the outcomes of learning may be convenient as a shorthand, it cannot be correct in any strict sense. A number of kinds of events may affect student performance at any given moment, but it is the underlying capability that is changed by learning. To be sure, observations of performance are what convince the instructor that a change in capability has taken place.

The difference between two performances in the same student is the observation employed to make the inference about a change in capability: at one time the student does not add two-digit numbers, and at another time he does.

But the aim of the instruction is to bring about the change in capability, and the observations made on performance must be carefully designed so that this inference can be made with confidence. The specific capabilities that are newly formed by learning can be described and classified in several different ways. Adding numbers, for instance, can be categorised as part of a larger set of capabilities in "whole number operations", which is part of a still larger set sometimes referred to as "arithmetic," which, in turn, forms a part of "mathematics." Forming correctly structured English sentences may be classified as a capability belonging to the larger class of "grammar," or of "language arts." Accordingly, one can, if he wishes, design a technology of instruction that is broken down into such subject-matter categories, as in "mathematics instruction," "English instruction," "science instruction," and so on. But it is evident from common usage that there must be a set of instructional categories that cuts across subject-matters. Thus, one thinks of instruction designed to establish knowledge of facts, whether these be facts of natural science, history, or mathematics.

Similarly, it is not uncommon to find consideration given to the learning of concepts, whether language concepts or science concepts; or to problems, solving whether in mathematics or social studies. Phrases of this sort imply that designers of instruction, and teachers, commonly think of categories of human capability as organised along dimensions which are independent of subject-matter. There seems to be different kinds of learning, each of which requires, in certain respects, a different kind of instruction. The view that categories of acquired capabilities may be distinguished in terms of the way they are observed or measured (that is, the kinds of performances to which they lead), as well as in terms of the kinds of change they imply, has been previously described (Gagne, 1965a, 1967).

1. *S-R Connections.* These are simple unitary motor acts that are usually acquired very early in the child's life, but some of which may be learned during school years. Making a mark on a piece of paper is an example; as is pronouncing the letter "I." For the most part, early school instruction simply assumes such capabilities as these.

2. *Discrimination.* Often, several simple connections must be learned so that different responses are made to different parts of the stimuli impinging on the learner. The performance to be observed is that of *distinguishing* colours, brightnesses, shapes, sizes, sounds, or various other portions of the environment. For example, the child must learn that the printed letter d is associated with the sound "duh," and also that printed letter b is associated with the sound "buh." He must not only acquire the two individual connections, he should not get them mixed up. Acquiring multiple discriminations is a matter of learning the capability of making a number of differential responses to an equivalent number of different stimulus categories.

3. *Motor Chains.* Integrated motor activities such as tying shoe-laces, printing letters, describing circles with a compass, focusing a miscroscope, and many others, are frequently capability of learned in school. A motor chain may be described as the carrying out a sequence of movements leading to a specifiable class of resulting in the environment of the learner. Printing a letter, drawing a circle, opening a lock, pronouncing a previously unfamiliar foreign word, are all examples of motor chains.

4. *Verbal Chains.* A good many verbal sequences are learned in school, and appear to underline the learning of

more complex verbal and intellectual skills. The young child learns to say the names of the numerals one to ten in order, and he may also learn the alphabet as a sequence. In addition, he acquires many common phrases, such as "boy and girl," "back and forth" "yes I will," and many others. Even later, verbal chains such as "one point four one four" may be a small but useful capability learned in mathematics. Considerably longer verbal chains, such as verses of songs or poetry, may also be learned as a part of school instruction. As a capability, a verbal chain is reflected in the performance of reinstating a sequences of verbal entities (usually words) which in its totality represents a specifiable outcome (the alphabet, a particular phrase or stanza).

5. *Concepts.* The most basic kinds of concepts appear to be capabilities of classifying objects (chair, table); events (expanding, contracting); or spatial and temporary relations up, down, before, after) into categories. What is notable about such classes that the physical appearance of their members may vary tremendously (a table, for example, may be large or small, high or low, three-legged or four-legged, and so on), yet the concept makes possible an identical response to them. Many fundamental concepts appear to be acquired by direct interaction of the learner with members of the class of objects or events concerned, and without the use of language. Other more abstract concepts (like "uncle," or "symmetry") are apparently most readily learned by means of language which itself refers to simpler concepts. In other words, they are learned by definition (cf. Gagne 1965 b, 1960a).

6. *Principles.* Another large class of learner capabilities reflected in school learning consists of principles or rules. Generally speaking, principles are combinations of concepts.

They may be represented by such simple sentences as "Water pours," or by such complex ones as "When a body is in equilibrium, the sum of the movements of force about an axis of rotation is equal to zero." It needs to be emphasised that a principle is an idea, or perhaps a set of ideas, but is not the verbal statement of the idea. The latter merely *represents* the principle. Obviously, a verbal statement may be learned as a verbal chain, but this capability is different from the capability usually meant by "knowing a principle."

A great deal of systematic knowledge acquired in the school situation consists of principles. As the psycholinguists have frequently pointed out, the learning of principles governing the use of language beings in early childhood (cf. Brown and Fraser, 1963). The child does not undertake the learning of the principles of syntax deliberately, but learn them he does, as can easily be proved by his performance in using them to communicate. Many kinds of principles are acquired in much the same way during the ordinary lifetime of the individual, which many others are learned as a result of formally planned instruction in the school. Principles are frequently arrived at by the individual himself, in a largely self-instructional manner, as a result of a kind of performance called *problem solving*. In this activity, the individual learner "discovers" a relationship among concepts or principles which leads to the acquisition of a "higher-order principle" (cf. Gagne, 1966b).

7. *Strategies.* Another kind of capability, which may be considered a variety of principle in its essential nature, is called a strategy, and is emphasised in the work of Bruner (1961), among others. A strategy is a principle governing choices of the individual's own actions. Thus, an individual

may acquire a strategy of solving algebra problems, or a strategy of persuading his parents, or strategy of investing his money. This kind of higher order principle is likely to be a higher generalisable capability (or so it is thought by many writers), and therefore to pervade a great many different aspects of his intellectual life. Behaving "creativity" may perhaps best be viewed as a matter of performing in accordance with certain previously learned strategies.

Notable, there are, then, six or seven *different* classes of capabilities that are acquired by the human learner during the course of his lifetime. Not only to these differ in indicating the variety of things an individual can do, they differ also in terms of the *conditions required for their learning* (Gagne, 1965a). The conditions for learning any single type of capability vary in respect to both the internal conditions of the learner (the state of his nervous system, including memorial traces), and the external conditions surrounding him and impinging upon him.

These external conditions as a whole constitute instruction and, accordingly, they are centrally involved in the question of how communication is related to learning. It is easy to choose extreme examples to demonstrate that the conditions for learning one type of capability differ markedly from those required in the learning of another type. The learning of a motor skill like batting a baseball, for example, is markedly little influenced by verbal communications on "how to do it," whereas it is strongly affected by a regime of practice with knowledge of results. In contrast, the basic rules of the game of baseball, although they could be incidentally acquired during long periods of practice and watching, are most readily and rapidly learned by being verbally communicated.

The sharp contrast provided by these particular

instances of learning is not an exceptional one. Rather, it is a familiar illustration of the general rule that learning different capabilities requires different conditions. The external components of these different sets of learning conditions are what must be identified in exploring the role of communication in learning.

The external conditions of learning may be said to embody the various kinds of communication made to the learner during the period of instruction. In this context, communication is meant in quite a broad sense. It often takes the form of verbal statements delivered to the learner in a language with which he is familiar. Frequently, communication assumes the form of printed or written statements in the familiar language. It may be noted that either of these forms may be mediated by a teacher (speaking/ or writing on a blackboard), or alternatively, by a device (a tape recorder or printed book). Pictures constitute another major category of communication available to the learner.

These may be still or moving; and there are many ways to present them (slides, film, television). A somewhat specialised form of communication is comprised nonlinguistic symbols, a form particularly relevant to the learning of such subjects as mathematics, science, and music. Other types of communication, including gestures and visual art, have even more highly restricted and specialised uses as part of instruction. The important question to be answered about communication in relation to learning does not concern the medium that is used for communicating, but rather, what functions the communication serves. The various conditions required for different forms of learning partake of communication in various ways. At any given moment during a period of instruction, the communication to the learner is fulfilling a function different from that of any other moment. It is necessary, therefore, to address the question of what these various functions might be.

In the broad sense employed in this chapter, communication enters into every variety of learning described in the previous section. It would be possible to describe the specific functions of communication in the learning of S-R connections, multiple discriminations, motor and verbal chains. However, since such a large part of educationally relevant learning comprises concepts and principles (including strategies), the discussion which follows will give primary emphasis to these kinds of learning. It is impossible to analyse the instructional event into a number of component stages, occurring in an approximate time sequence. The functions of communication may most readily be described for each of these stages separately. First, communication to the learner may have the function of *gaining and controlling his attention.* Next, the *stimuli for learning* are to be presented. At some point early in instruction, the learner needs to be *informed of the required performance* he will be expected to exhibit after learning. Some sort of communication must be made to stimulate the learner in *recalling previously learned capabilities.* Now the stage is set essential act of learning, but in achieving this, one must often make provision for communication which accomplishes the *guidance of learning.*

Once the new capability has been initially attained, communication may *provide feedback* or confirmation of the learning. Finally, if the newly learned entity is to be broadly useful, provision must be made to promote the transfer of learning. The following paragraphs briefly describe how each of these parts of the instructional process may be influenced by communication.

The idea that the learner must attend to relevant

stimuli in the learning environment comes from an accumulation of instructional experience (James, 1958, pp. 77-86) as well as from modern evidence about the functioning of the brain (Berlyne, 1965, Lindsley, 1957). Whatever stimulus objects are to form a part of the learning event, whether they be actual objects, pictures, symbols, or words, they must have an initial *registration* effect in order for learning to occur. Essentially this means that they must be perceived, or coded, in some way that makes it possible for them to mediate the neural events necessary for learning. As a simple example, a word such as *flower,* when occurring in a printed communication, must in the usual instance of learning be registered as the referenced concept "flower," and not as merely a printed word. The young and undisciplined learner must acquire whole set of habits of attention in order to begin the process of learning. Original stimuli for the arousal of attention, which function also in the establishment of these basic attentional habits, are known to be such things as intense stimuli (loud sounds or bright flashes, for example); repeated stimuli, rapidly changing stimulation (movement or other forms of change); or objects which are associated with certain basic needs such as hunger and sex. As is well known, these same stimuli are widely employed as attention-gainers in advertising, in this case largely with mature and disciplined learners, whose attentional habits to certain products have become extinguished because these stimuli are encountered to frequently in the absence of need.

Under these circumstances, the basic attention-getters are used again and again in great variety to re-establish the desired attentional habits for intervals long enough for the advertisement, or a portion of it, to be perceived and its "message" to be learned. For these two classes of learners (those whose attentional habits are not yet established, and those whose attention has been extinguished), communication must take a particular form in order to arouse attention. It needs to be loud, varied, repeated, and perhaps associated with prepotent drives. For the young child, the state of arousal which leads to the establishment of attentional habits may take the form of relatively intense visual or auditory stimulation, supplied by a teacher or parent, or rapid movement and change as contained, for example, in a motion picture or television presentation.

Actually, this kind of attention-getting communication may take many forms, too numerous to catalog here. In any case, the intention which are eventually to be controlled by much less intense stimuli. According, which this purpose is being pursued, the intensive of the stimuli needs to be progressively reduced, in order that attention will be more readily controlled for purposes of subsequent learning. For the student who has acquired basic attentional habits related to the kind of stimuli normally encountered in school, there is, of course, no need to resort to communications having this markedly intensive character. Similarly, the disciplined adult learner whose need for learning is unambiguous, presents no requirement for communication of the intensive sort. Attention can readily be aroused in such learners by brief verbal directions such as "Now notice..." or "Look at the diagram...," or by symbols (arrows, etc.), or signals (beeps, etc.) which sometimes serve the same function in such media as motion pictures or recorded presentations. Under these circumstances, the maintenance of attention can generally be insured so long as the relation of the material to his wants or purposes is evident to the learner.

Ordinarily, one does not think of the learner's interaction

with relevant physical objects as falling into the category of communication. Yet, conditions of learning that include physical objects are on a continuum with those that include pictures or demonstrations, and the latter may usually be classed as instances of communication. Provided the learner has acquired suitable attention habits, as well as requisite picture-observing habits, the activity of observing demonstrations or pictures of demonstrations may be a highly effective substitute for reactions to real objects. For example, a well-designed demonstration (live or in motion pictures) of Archimedes' principle, or of the concept of a lever, may be quite as effective a condition of learning as requiring the student to manipulate objects directly, provided the student has had certain other kinds of prerequisite experiences. An important function of communication, then, may be to substitute for reality in representing concrete stimulus objects or events of the sort that are the direct objects of the behaviour being learned. This function of presenting the stimulus, it may be noted, is only a single step in the set of external events that is necessary to bring about learning. Yet, the existence of communication media which can represent and provide a substitute for the real thing enormously extends the range of possibilities for learning.

Many concepts of earth strata and rock formation can be learned via the communication of pictures; architectural features that characterise buildings in remote parts of the earth can be identified and classified by means of pictures. It would be of little use to attempt to multiply these few examples to emphasis a generalisation that obviously applies to virtually every field of study. Learning is extended to great limits by the use of pictures as media of communication even when one considers these as performing the restricted function of presenting stimuli. Similar considerations apply to moving pictures, quite irrespective of the system used to display them (movies, television, etc.).

Moving pictures are important means for communicating stimuli that embody motion, as in the case of the operation of engines, the movement of water, or the behaviour of animals. As is well known, they can also marvellously extend the range of possible events to be communicated, as in the speeded-up display of plant growth, the motion of planets, or the representation of historical events. The function of presenting the stimulus is also performed by communication which is verbal, using words and sentences. This is probably the most widely used method. The learner is presented with a sentence describing cell division, rather than with a picture or with the actual cells. The conditions of family life in colonial days are described rather than being pictured, and of course cannot be observed directly. The concept of potential energy is defined in sentences and equations, rather than being demonstrated or pictured.

The verbal means of communicating the stimulus for learning is relatively easy to use, and has virtually no limits at all with respect to what kinds of stimuli can be displayed. It may be noted that there are many media by means of which verbal communications may be presented. The human being in the person of an instructor or teacher comes first to mind, and in this case the representation of the stimulus is usually presented orally to the student in a direct, face-to-face manner. The same kind of stimulus presentation, virtually undiminished in effectiveness so far as this restricted function is concerned, may be carried out by speech recordings.

In printed or written form, an even wider variety of media way provide the learner with symbolic representations of the stimulus. These include the teacher's writing, printed pages of books or papers, and various forms of filmed or electronic displays of words and sentences. The sophisticated learner has little difficulty in learning concepts and principles, in any content field, under learning conditions that include verbal representations of stimuli. But the inexperienced learner may have serious difficulty. This is because the experienced learner is well aware that words are merely representations of reality; that it is the referents of the words which are the true stimuli, not the words themselves. The inexperienced learner may not have acquired this basic strategy, and therefore may fall into the trap of learning mere words of word-sequences.

The capability he acquires becomes that of a verbal chain, rather than a principle. He learns to give an answer to a verbal question, and is not able to respond correctly when confronted with reality. This is surely one important reason why pictures have advantages over words as representations of stimuli; they are less likely to lead the unsophisticated learner astray. This fact should probably not be used, however, as an argument against attempting to teach the unskilled learner to acquire the capability of responding properly to verbal presentations in learning.

Remarkably, another function performed by communication within a learning situation is informing the learner of what he will be able to do once he has learned. If a student is to learn a motor chain for printing an E, he is first shown a printed E. If he is to learn the concept of *cell nucleus,* he is first shown examples of the class of objects which are called cell nuclei. It appears that the procedure of giving the learner information about the expected performance (which he will be able to do after learning) may not be followed consistently in typical school learning. To the extent that this is so, a probably important function of communication is being neglected.

Suppose the learner is confronted with a passage in a textbook reading as follows: "The kinetic energy of a body moving with speed $v$ can be determined by calculating the work done in accelerating the body from rest to speed $v$. Since work, $W = Fs$, we can show by Newton's second law, $F = ma$ that $W = mas$, or $W = 1/2\ mv^2$. That is, the work done in accelerating the body is equal to the change in its kinetic energy, or $E_k = ½mv^2$." It is evident that this communication, by itself, does not inform the learner of what he is expected to learn. Several different requirements are possible, including:

1. stating that work done in accelerating a body is or is not equal to the change in its kinetic energy;
2. calculating the change in kinetic energy of a body, given the mass and velocity associated with the change;
3. demonstrating that the change in kinetic energy of a body is equal to the work done on the body.

In fact, in view of the fact that each of these possibilities requires the learning of a somewhat different set of principles, it is not difficult to understand the need for telling the learner which of the performances, or what combinations of them, he is expected to acquire. In practice, this kind of communication may have been given to the student at the beginning of a course, or in the early pages of a textbook, so that it does not have to be repeated in connection with each new stimulus presentation. Too frequently, however, this kind of information is not systematically included as a part of the learning situation.

Arousing attention, presenting the relevant stimuli, and informing the learned about his expected performance, are all early events in the process of instruction. But there is still another communication function which may sometimes precede these in time. This is the stimulation of recall of capabilities that have been previously learned, and which are essential components of the new learning about to occur.

Learning a concept, for example, requires the recall of discriminations which differentiate positive and negative instances of the class of objects conceptualised: learning the concept of a rectangle involves recall of the discrimination of inequality of lengths of sides. Similarly, learning a principle takes place under conditions in which the learner recalls previously learned concepts or simpler principles. Before the learning occurs, communication may be necessary to arouse the recall of these previously learned entities.

At some point in an instructional sequence, communication may be employed to guide learning. Typically, verbal statements or questions are presented which determine the direction of the learner's internal intellectual processes, although there are occasions when pictures or symbols may perform this function equally well or better. The effect of such communication is to permit the learner to arrive at the new principle without wasting his time considering possibilities which are wrong in extreme degree (cf. Gagne and Brown, 1961). The function of guidance is perhaps most strikingly illustrated under conditions in which the learner is expected to arrive at a new principle by problem solving. For example, in one of Katona's (1940) studies the learners were asked to learn to perform a card trick. The correct performance of the trick results in alternate red and black cards being placed in order on the table, when successive cards from the top of the deck are dealt alternatively to the table and to the bottom of the deck. The principle being learned is one which makes possible the arranging of the deck so that this result will be achieved. In this study, a blackboard demonstration was employed to guide the learning. During the demonstration, the known and unknown cards were displayed on the board in a sequence, the unknown ones being represented by question marks. Instructions were given which led the learners to examine each of these questions in a systematic order, unit they discovered for themselves the principle involved in arranging the cards.

The experiments showed that subjects instructed in this way retained the capability of performing the card trick, and variations of it, much better than did subjects who memorised the order of the cards. The amount of guidance provide by instructions can obviously be varied within a wide range. When little is given, instruction is said to emphasise discover (Gagne, 1966b). At the other end of the spectrum, the principle to be learned may be stated verbally, thus providing a maximum amount of guidance. Such a method of didactic instruction is one which is often used (most textbooks are written that way), and is usually one of the most rapid methods of learning for the experienced learner. Methods with intermediate amounts of learning guidance, called guided discover, have been shown in some studies to yield better retention principles (Wittrock, 1966).

Basically, the learner often need a kind of communication that provides him with feedback, or confirmation that he has managed to acquire the new capability. If he is acquiring the concept of *gas* as a state of matter, he may need to be told the correctness of this identification of the bubbles arising out of a boiling liquid as a gas. If he is learning a principle relating potential energy to mass and velocity, he may need to be told the correctness of his identification of the amount of potential energy possessed by a specific body in a specific situation. Feedback has the effect of preventing the retention of incorrectly learned acts.

More importantly, in the view of many students of the learning process, it provides reinforcement, and thus tends to perpetuate what is learned. Although there are undoubtedly instances in which pictorial media could be used to some advantage for purposes of providing feedback, this communication function is typically conducted by verbal means, either printed or oral.

One of the most important varieties of feedback communication is that which occurs during instructional periods that are dynamic in the sense that the feedback is graded and selected according to the degree or quality of correctness of the student's response. Interchanges between the individual student and the teacher are likely to have this characteristics, and such a quality of instruction is often aimed for in the seminar or free-discussion group. In dynamic instruction of this sort, the student's attempts at problem solving can be subjected to many gradations of feedback, and in this manner his newly conceived ideas can be refined and sharpened in a highly selective and individual manner. It seems unlikely that the personal interaction involved in this form of instruction can ever be fully supplanted by any combination of mechanical communication media. Most experienced teachers are highly cognizant of the peculiar value of this form of instruction. Such an evaluation, however, need not blind one to the fact that there is a great deal of necessary instruction which does not need to be of the dynamic sort.

A final function of communication to be described is the promotion of transfer of learning from the immediate instructional situation to new tasks of learning both inside and outside of the school situation. Learned capabilities are useful to the individual to the extent that they can be generalised in their application to subsequent learning or to the performance of a variety of practical tasks.

In serving this function, communication takes the form of providing a variety of examples, or a variety of opportunities for application of newly acquired knowledge. A principle such as that of proportional representation in legislative bodies, for instance, may need to be demonstrated by the student in a number of specific examples pertaining to nations, states, and local governments, in order to insure its generalisability to subsequent learning or to the activities of a citizen. Most often, such additional instances are provided by verbal descriptions made by a teacher or textbook. Again, other media can perhaps be of value, but hardly of unique importance in the presentation of this kind of instruction. It appears that oratory communications are of little value in "instruction for transfer." The student may be made aware of the necessity for generalising his newly learned capabilities, but is unable to do so simply as a result of urging. General communications of the sort "Keep this in mind always," or 'Be careful" have never been demonstrated to be effective in generating transfer to new situations.

It may be noted that a considerable portion of the total communication in this example is concerned with preparation for the learning act (controlling attention, recalling previously learned principles) and that a fairly substantial amount pertains to events subsequent to the learning itself (feedback, promotion of transfer). This leaves a relatively small portion of the total message to deal with presentation of the essential stimulus and the guidance of learning. Insofar as this division of function is concerned, this is probably a quite typical instance.

Certain kinds of communication of the sort identified in the table might be omitted for the experienced learner. For example, it might not be necessary to gain attention in such an obvious fashion. Direct reminders of what has been learned previously might not have to be given. In addition, guidance of learning might be omitted or at least reduced to the barest hint.

**Media of Communication**

Some implications of this analysis of the functions of communication for learning may now be drawn. Of particular significance, perhaps, are the conclusions suggested regarding the important problem of choosing communication media for instruction.

For a number of years, investigators of the uses and effectiveness of communication media in instruction have pursued certain research questions vigorously (cf. Hoban and VanOrmer, 1950; May and Lumsdaine, 1958). One of these has been the question: Which medium, or combination of media, is best for teaching mathematics? or chemistry? or history? It is well known that these investigations have generally not yielded consistent findings. Sometimes motion pictures have been found to be advantageous as compared, say, to a lecture, and sometimes not. Sometimes recorded speech has been found to be effective for learning, as compared with a live teacher, and sometimes not. The answers obtained do not seem to be any more consistent with one kind of subject matter than with another. The implication of the present analysis is clearly that dependable answers to the question of matching particular subject matter with particular media are unlikely to be obtained except in highly specialised instances.

There are to reasons for this. The first is that a number of functions of communications in learning might be equally well performed by any medium. For example, it is difficult to think of a reason why stimulus presentation which requires verbal statement could be performed with differential effectiveness by a teacher's written statement on a blackboard, by a printed statement in a text-book, or by a printed statement projected on a television screen. Similarly, on what basis could one suppose an advantages for the rural reminder of a teacher versus the pictorial reminder of a projected film sequence, in stimulating recall of previously learned concepts? The second reason why matching subject-matter and media seems an infeasible task resides in the fact that a medium well adapted for one communication function may be ill-adapted for a second and different function within the same instructional sequence.

For example, in a lesson concerned with mechanical advantage, pictures may be well suited for the function of recalling to the learner previously learned concepts concerning the length of lever arms, but quite ineffective in presenting the stimulus and guiding learning for the principle $F_1 X d_1 = F_2 X d_2$. Thus any advantage which accrues in learning from the performance of the first function pictorially may well be cancelled by a disadvantage of using pictures to perform the second function.

Highly similar considerations would seem to apply to the related attempt to seek an answer to the question of matching media and learners (cf. Lumsdaine and May,

1965). Generally speaking, the idea that "some people learn better from pictures" has by no means received any marked amount of confirmation from studies carried out over a period of years. Again, the possibility suggested by the present analysis is that while some communication *functions* may be better performed by particular media for particular kinds of learners, other functions within a single instructional sequence may not be. For example, a highly verbal learner may be able to translate a picture into a verbal statement of the stimulus situation quite readily, whereas an individual of low verbal ability may not. Quote the reverse may be true, however, if the function to be performed by the picture is the recall of previously learned concepts. Thus, a consistent answer to the question of who learns best from pictures, where learning refers to a total sequence of instruction, may be unreasonable to expect.

The suggested route to the continued search for a match between communication media and effective learning is through a process of analysis of the sort previously described. In making such an analysis, several steps are necessary, which may be described as follows:

1. It is essential to determine what kind of capability is to be learned, is it a verbal chain? a motor chain? a concept? a principle? a strategy? The characteristics of these learned entities have been briefly described in an earlier section and more fully elsewhere (Gagne, 1965).
2. The requirements that each type of learning imposes on the process of instruction need to be described. Concept learning, for example, requires the recall of a different type of previously acquired capability than does principle learning. Practice means something quite different in verbal chain learning

and in concept learning. A more extensive treatment of these points may be found in Gagne (1967).

3. The functions which can or should be performed by communication within the instructional situation must be differentiated, in the manner previously described An extensive discussion of this procedure and its relation to the choice of media is contained in a report by Briggs, Campeau, Gagne, and May (1966).
4. An instructional sequence incorporating these communicating functions may be designed, identifying the medium or media which are best suited to perform each of these functions.
5. If a choice of a single medium is to be made, or a combination of media, this may be done by selecting the ones which can serve as vehicles for the various communication functions without having conflicting effects on the instruction to be undertaken.

After disthe theoretical approaches to communication, now we will proceed to elucidate communications revolution and its impact on mass communication today.

# 4

# The Communications Revolution

"It is a thousand times better to have common sense without education than to have education without common sense."

—*R.G. Ingersoll*

Today, however—in the midst of social and technological explosions in various fields of knowledge, as well as in the techniques by which this burgeoning knowledge is communicated—the teacher can no longer attempt to be the sole information-giving instrument in the classroom. Indeed the teacher himself can no longer keep pace with the expanding world of information. Further, the growing school population and its concomitantly larger and more diverse variety of classes make it increasingly more difficult for a single teacher to reach individual pupils with traditional classroom information-giving methods. These methods, what is more, fail to compete with the increasing variety of up-to-date communication techniques to which pupils are exposed outside of school, and even long before they enter school at all. In other words, in our truly remarkable age, the task of effective teaching becomes ever more difficult. Let us examine some of the impediments to efficient teaching and learning which have derived from our modern world.

Never before has our population grown so rapidly by

percentage or by sheet numbers. Naturally, the school population, too, increases as the population of the United States leaps ahead. In addition to the national population growth, however, is the fact that more and more of out school-age children are actually attending school. Since 1930, practically all of our children of elementary school age have been enrolled in school, and there has been an enormous leap in school enrollment at the high-school level. In 1930 only 47 percent of our high school youth were enrolled in secondary schools, while 1950 saw 83 percent of this age group enrolled in secondary schools; by 1974 it is estimated that this enrollment will approach 100 percent of educable high-school-aged youth. The upsurge in education is also reflected in the increase in the proportion of pupils who actually graduate from high school and those who seek entrance to collage.

Never in the history of this country has so large a proportion of our children wanted or been able to continue their education. The changing numbers of pupils in public elementary and high schools are set forth. During the ten-year period 1955-1965, elementary enrollment rose over five millions from 21.8 to 27.1 millions. During the same period, high school enrollment nearly doubled from 8.2 to 15.7 millions. These increase in our school population have complicated the problems of instruction. Larger classes present particular burdens to teachers who are less and less able to relate to individual pupils and their needs. Arranging suitable learning experiences and utilising interesting communications techniques that will challenge an ever-widening array of interests, background, and abilities are formidable tasks. Clearly, to meet these teaching challenges, the best of an increasingly diverse availability of tools must be utilised, particularly those tools by which information is communicated to the learners.

As the explosion of knowledge continues, teachers are being assigned newer subject-area teaching responsibilities. There is more and more to know, more of social importance, more of scientific and technological importance and more experience which the learner must be given before he can assume full and desirable social participation in the rapidly expanding world of today and tomorrow. New developments in social studies and science, etc., are far beyond the experience of the teacher who was trained even five years ago. Today, for example teachers must guide learners toward information about areas of the world never included in the older, Europe-oriented social studies curriculum. Information advances in vocational arts, home economics, sports, recreation, health safety, etc. show similar trends.

Today's teachers are also confronted with keeping abreast of rapid changes occurring in the area of social studies. Consider, for example, the current need for understanding Hong Kong—the international settlement which last year produced more entertainment motion-picture films than the United States-and for understanding the affairs of communist china, as well as the Nationalist Chinese activities on the island of Formosa. The pupil of today is barely beginning to be aware of the 700. Islands of the Philippines, with its 30 million people who are working industriously to release its immeasurable natural resources. These resources are only now undergoing modern-day industrial development. Australia and New Zealand, too are no longer distant and little-known "down under" countries: rather, they are emerging as highly industrialised complexes which are carrying forward social planning of the most advanced order.

The trust territories of the South Pacific, long neglected, are now receiving attention from the Congress of the United

States, and American Samoa is the site of the most modern educational television installation in the world. Indeed, the pupil of today is no longer preoccupied with European social studies backgrounds but turns his attention more and more to the East. One reason is that this area, which contains the world's greatest concentration of population, is awakening and making tremendous strides in communication and transportation. Japan, home for one hundred million people is only one example of this new focus on the East. Japan is rushing into the modern American curriculum in new "grab". This Island nation has achieved the world's greatest increase in annual gross national product for five years running.

Today, that country annually launches more new ocean-vessel tonnage than any other country in the world. Education television is more universal than in the United States. Japanese winter sports and recreational facilities are bourgeoning at a tremendous rate. Yet, how many teachers still retain the impression of Japan as a quaint, leisurely, cherry blossom-bedecked Island nation of strange people and customs? At the East-West Center, University of Hawaii, a new teacher interchange programme is in progress. Social-studies teachers representing United States mainland school districts are invited to study side by side with social-studies teachers who represent such Asian countries and territories as Japan, Formosa, Hong Kong, and Thailand as well as India, Australia, New Zealand, and Maxico. In analysing the progress of this project, professor Ronald Anderson reports. "The speed with which pacific nations are growing in industrialisation population and communication is almost unbelievable. It is high time that Asian social studies courses are included in mainland U.S. high school curricula."

The situation which Dr. Anderson reports is typical of the dilemma not only in history and social studies, but in every area where the information explosion has been taking place. Today the world is in a state of change and the nature of these changes must be known first to those who teach if it is to be passed on to those who learn.

The knowledge explosion and the changing social world of man are reflected in curriculum changes in our schools. A half century ago, the curriculum was rather rigidly represented by 24 subject units in the fields of grammar, Latin, mathematics, history and rhetoric. By contrast in 1962, the United States Office of Education released the results of a survey on *what High School pupils study*. A wide sampling of American high-school students reported their enrollment in nearly 1000 distinct and identifiable courses.:

| | |
|---|---|
| English 137 | Music 82 |
| Mathematics 91 | Home Economics 73 |
| Foreign Language 44 | Business 143 |
| Science 74 | Health and Physical Education 87 |
| Social Studies 203 | Vocational Education 65 |
| | Unclassified 73 |

In other words, the school today finds itself with more and more subject information to teach. Of necessity, the child spends more time in school. Yet a dilemma is unfolding. "No longer can one small head [that of the teacher] carry all that a student must learn. We must do something drastic to better enable us to handle the staggering build-up of new knowledge."[3] Nor can the chief instructional medium, the textbook, be relied upon much longer to communicate with efficiency. This does not mean that to understand this new information our old techniques should be eliminated; rather, something must be done about the means of using new communication techniques-educational media-to "backstop" the teacher in his task of communicating current, useful, and accurate information to learners. New instructional materials must be utilised in sufficient measure to provide pupils with the needed concrete, or quasi-concrete, experiences on the basis of which both old and new material may be made understandable. It is only in the very newest instructional materials-films, filmstrips, sliders, charts, models and other audio visual media-that adequate experience with the modern world may be provided.

Ironically, the increasingly difficult task that confronts today's teacher is further complicated by the mushrooming availability of these new and novel educational media. A sizable portion of these depend on reading skills for interpretation. Table 5.1 outlines graphically the explosion of knowledge as it has been made available to teachers and pupils in textbook form alone. In addition to an increasing array of standard textbooks, however, new formats-including paperback books, cluster systems of series of related booklets, and programmed materials and texts-are being put on the educational market virtually everyday. As one teacher exclaimed on his return from the district convention, "I've never seen such a collection of books and reference materials-I could spend weeks just leafing through what's new in my subject alone!" The reading load this avalanche of new printed materials represents to the teacher is made all the more difficult by the teacher's task of interpreting this material accurately for the pupil. A district or regional media center also becomes the repository for professional materials, both print and non-print, in quantities impossible for one school to house. These resources enable professional personnel to engage in extended research and study either at the center or in their own school.

Center services also extend to in-service education activities related to the design, production and utilisation of instructional media. Again, these activities can be carried on either in the center or individual schools.

In addition to providing in service education activities for the professional staff, the central office should assist the school by providing activities for the technical clerical staff. Workshops for non-professional personnel include instruction in finding and making instructional materials and in assisting the media specialists and teachers. School systems which are experimenting with new and innovative kinds of programmes should be identified and arrangements made for both teachers and media specialists to visit and observe activities which may be adapted to improve their own programmes. Perhaps the most important service of the center is its consultant and supervisory assistance to schools in their efforts to develop exciting and imaginative programmes.

Planning new or remodelled facilities for school media centers represents another area of the media specialist's responsibility. School planners and media specialists must work together in order to be sure that adequate facilities to accommodate media programmes are included when remodelling or building a new school. Supervisors can provide information on current trends in media service, on the way media centers operate in the instructional programmes of the school, and how these facilities will implement the instructional programme. As the school facilities and programme grow, center personnel should take an active role in recruiting specialists, technicians, and clerks; assist the personnel department in interviewing candidates for positions; and in advising principals in assigning successful candidates to positions.

Programme planning at the school-system level provides the framework in which local planning can proceed. One helpful element in such system wide planning is the development of standards for local school media services. Local standards designed to meet local needs or problems provide specific short-term goals and assistance in developing budgets. The district media center staff should prepare a staffing formula to meet local needs and to provide for a growing programme. Such standards provide guidelines for developing the programme, and they also serve to inform the local superintendent and board of education of the needs of the media programme. The preparation of regular progress reports for presentation to the superintendent and board are necessary to keep them informed about the development of school media services in both the district and in individual schools. When needed the district center should prepare special reports in order to inform the school board and the general public of the importance of the media programme or to develop and justify the annual budget. The center's media supervisors should visit schools frequently to assist media specialists, teachers, and principals in developing long-range plans for improving media services and the instructional programme itself. Supervisors should meet with the faculty members in individual schools to assist in solving problems in their programmes and to remind them of the services available from the school system media center.

These consultation visits give the supervisors a further opportunity to discuss new development in instructional media and help local building personnel increase their competencies in teaching and in the use of instructional materials and equipment. The regional media center can assist the local school in identifying useful materials for instruction by setting up a review and examination service through the center. Teachers and media specialists working with instructional supervisors, can examine, subject by subject, the materials needed in the various programmes. They can eliminate for the whole school system those which are *obviously* not worhty of consideration by the individual schools. The district media center can then assemble requested materials for preview and examination by all of the schools.

Using the evaluations provided by small groups of teachers and media specialists, the district media center can issue lists of recommended materials which have been identified as useful in supporting the school district curriculum. These materials provide both media specialists and teachers an opportunity to examine materials of known value in order to select those which will prove useful in meeting the needs of individual students and of specific school programmes. In order to do this, teachers will need released time for this work. The district materials center may provide even more complex services, such as radio and television and dial-access retrieval services. These services should supplement those of the individual school. In effect, the district media center bears the same relationship to the school media center that the school media center does to the classroom. Whether local or regional, media centers exist for only one purpose: to promote more effective teaching and learning. They supply the materials and equipment which support instructions, facilities for their use, and most important of all, competent media personnel to assist students and teachers in using media as they study and teach.

The media center provides the organisational unit through which the varied media of communication can have impact on the educational programme. If man's landing on the moon is the greatest miracle of planning and coordination, dedication and will-power of any human endeavour, we sometimes wonder if our capability to see him do it and communicate with him at all stages of this incredible achievement is not a greater miracle! It is not as if we had to watch this fantastic happening through some expensive complicated instrument in an observatory or some such place aided by a dozen experts and get a vague and distant impression of something happening somewhere, and take their word for it that what you supposed to have seen was the real thing. Not at all. You sit down in your favourite chair in the drawing-room, pour yourself a drink if you like, light a cigarette, dim the lights and ask your daughter to turn on the TV. And there you are! Mr. Armstrong himself looking at you, talking to you, with the dark, cold landscape of the moon as his background.

In a few moments, he is ready to start his journey back to earth. And the smallest mistake will be not merely the end of Mr. Armstròng but of the hopes of science and the hopes of the whole world. And we hold our breath. Science must win. Human will must conquer. And as we watch, man and science triumph. And what a victory!

There are two important points. One is the triumph of science- the invention, the development, the refinement of a new technology in communication. The other is a kind of 'happening' the like of which has never before happened in the history of man. For a few minutes some four hundred million people, an eighth of the population of this world, watched one event, concentrated on the same thing and simultaneously heaved a sigh of relief and joy. For a few minutes the world was like one global village, like one family. It was a fantastic demonstration of true "fellow-felling", the capacity of man to feel for man. And the world will not be the same ever again, in spite of all our recurring strains and tensions and our capacity for hatred.

That too was television, and like the gigantic moon-landing programme, a shared experience though on an infinitely smaller scale. This is the real miracle of television: the involvement of the viewer in what he watches. In both these cases, it was a case of history being made, right there in front of the viewer-a participant in the event. You could read about it in hundreds of papers the next morning, see it on the screen of thousands of cinemas a day later, but, by then you are a detached observer no longer a participant. The event has taken place, you know about it you appreciate the skill with which the event has been reconstructed for you, but the historic moment has long been over and you are not a part of it.

The real excitement of television is this shared experience, whether it is the landing on the moon, the tension of a football match the marriage of a princess, the coronation of a queen, the risks taken by a daring young man on the flying trapeze. Everything happens right in front of you, and you are involved. You can recreate something of this tension in the theatre in the cinema, but that would be the result of a willing suspension of disbelief. But as you watch television you watch the whole world at work play, then and there, participate in historic events of every kind. And it adds a whole dimension to your life and experience, transforming you into a different kind of human being.

Are we talking of communication? Can it do all this? Add a whole new dimension to your life? Can it transform you into a different kind of human being?

In the beginning was the word, but the word was

spoken. Then came the invention of writing which froze the spoken word into a visual shape and changed the character and basis of language. Next came printing, which gave the written word a mass basis, creating two types of languages-the spoken and the written-and two types of human beings, the illiterate and the literate. And next broadcasting and the electronic media, making the dissemination of information and ideas, of sound and pictures on a scale so gigantic and global that no one is immune from it. We are still in the middle of it all to realise what is happening to us. Now let us take communication in another sense-'access or means of access between two or more persons or places.' Two early revolutionary developments were the invention of the wheel and the capture and taming of the horse. For several millenniums nothing more happened until the invention of the steam engine; then quite soon after, of the internal combustion engine, and before we knew what was what the jet. In some one hundred and fifty years-what a minute span it represents in the development of the human species-we had jumped from the speed of a horse, to 18,000 miles an hour the speed at which Mr. Armstrong shot out to the moon.

There would seem to be close parallels in these two separate developments in communication and they are worth examining.

The human species must have spent several millenniums trying to communicate with one another-crying, grunting, roaring, laughing, gesticulating. And out of these sounds and in very slow measure, must have emerged sounds which were identified with objects and animals and trees, and action of all kinds, then thoughts and deeds and feelings. And when the spoken word was formed it must been the noblest sound, the most valuable instrument that man ever created. And in this process of creation one can sense the close relationship between sound and symbol and meaning. Sound is more elemental than meaning. The word is revealed to us first as sound. The registration of the meaning occurs a split second late on a different plane. The element force, the expression, which lies behind the sound of a word is lost when it is spelt out on a page. It is this elemental sound which is behind the power of oratory, of declamation, and which affects the listener more directly than the meaning. As Arnheim once put it," The pure sound in the word is the Mother Earth from which the spoken work of art must never cut loose." This new mode of communication—the noblest sound created by man—must have grown and must have been refined to the limit of man's capacity wherever he was over a long, long period.

And depending on his environment, his needs, his physical features, living speech must have taken on different sounds, different nuances and stresses in different nooks and corners of this wide world. How little do we know of all this? When did man start to talk? Which community started it and where? What were the high peaks of sophistication and refinement achieved? We don't know, until recorded history gives us some clues. But 'records' imply writing and the world of the spoken word would have by then vanished.

Basically, language of some of the great epics, of pronouncements, of dialogues from before the days of writing which have been passed on to us by word of mouth, through oral communication and finally preserved later on by the written word-the wisdom of Socrates the *Upanisbads* of India, the *Iliad* of Homer, the 'J' narratives in *Genesis*. These works communicate to us in a different way from the written books of later days. They need a different approach if we are to get their full impact. The words are in a different order. They are less abstract, less intellectual. It is difficult, if not impossible for us, to understand, even to imagine, what must have gone on in the minds of people who spoke, and of those who listened, before writing was invented. They must have had a different apparatus of communication, both of speaking and of listening. This explains some of our difficulties in comprehending Homer, or Socrates.

They have to be read aloud and listened to with a different kind of focus. At the time that writing was invented, it was not considered an unmixed blessing. We know the story attributed to Socrates, attributed by Plato. We must remember that Plato *wrote,* while Socrates *spoke,* and one can sense a kind of mischievous, slightly malicious antagonism in Plato's reportage.

"I heard", says Socrates, or so Plato reports on Socrates, "that there in Egypt was one of the ancient gods of that country, the one whose sacred bird is the Ibis, and the name of the god himself was Theuth. He it was who invented numbers and arithmetic and astronomy, also draughts and dice, and most important of all, *letters.* Now the king of all Egypt at that time was the god Thamus....... To him came Theuth to show his inventions, saying that they ought to be imparted to all Egyptians. But Thamus asked what use there was in each......and expressed praise or blame as he approved or disapproved....... When they came to the letters, 'this invention, O King,' said Theuth, 'will make Egyptians wiser and will improve their memories; for it is an elixir of memory and wisdom that I have discovered.' But Thamus replied, `Most ingenious Theuth, one man has the ability to beget arts, but to judge of the good or evil they will do, belongs to another; and now you, who are the father of letters, have been led by your affection to ascribe to them a power the opposite of that which they really possess....... You offer your pupils the appearance of wisdom only...for they will read many things without instruction and will *seem* to *know*, when they are for the most part ignorant and hard to get along with.'"

Socrates continues, "He who thinks that he has left any work behind him in writing, and he who receives it in the belief that anything in writing will be clear and certain, would be an utterly simple person....... Every word when once it is written, is bandied about alike among those who understand and those who have no interest in it.....for it has no power to protect or help itself."

"Instead of such words," continues Socrates, "instead of such words, the true teacher will use the legitimate brother of this bastard sort of speech......and sow in a fitting soul intelligent words which are able to help themselves and him who planted them......words which are not fruitless, but yield seed from which there spring up in other minds other words continuing the process for ever, and making their possessor happy to the last possible limit of human happiness."

This story is from *Phaedrus* and the point developed here was brought into focus by Professor I.A. Richards in a broadcast from the Third Programme of the B.B.C., about thirty five years ago or so, long back. Marshall McLuhan also deals with it in *The Gutenberg Galaxy* (1962) and *The Medium is the Massage* (1967). Richards was speculating on the differences between the spoken word and the written word, between speech and writing. His enquiring mind analysed this with such perception that I cannot resist the temptation of quoting him at some length.

"Silent reading," suggested Richards, "is an anti-social activity. When St. Augustine first saw a man reading to himself silently (it was St. Ambrose) he was deeply shocked. He knew Ambrose was a good man, what he did couldn't be wicked..... but still listening, in contrast, tends to communality. What is listened to, by choice, in common, speaks, it is assumed, to `the all in each in all men.' This may be low and trivial. But it may, as the *Iliad* and the earliest verse and prose of the Bible remind us, deal with man's highest and most momentous concerns.

"The *Iliad* and the pre-writing narratives of the Old Testament were products of public competition. They were the winners, the things which best pleased, and continued to please, their audiences through a centuries-long series of elimination trials. I do not think it is being sentimental or romantic or nostalgic to stand in some awe of the critical judgement of these early audiences who listened and judged Homer and the 'J' narratives of *Genesis.* They had this advantage over us. They were expert audiences, experienced in what they judged. They knew the stories. The form and style they were told in, had been settled. The audiences knew in general what to expert....... So they could concentrate on how well it was done. They did not have to wonder what sort of a game this was, or what the rules, if any, were, or what the player was trying to do. They knew all that, and could devote themselves to judging the play.

"The result was a sort of economical functional efficiency....... Furthermore, the *Iliad* is a collective product, in shaping which the expressed preferences of the audience, expressed then and there, had an immediate effect on the poets. Kipling puts it beautifully, `Unless they pleas, they are not heard at all'.....

"Then, into this mode of composition came the new influence of writing. As to how it came in—that is all speculation. Early inventions often spread slowly and unevenly. Probably writing was used in commerce for centuries before poets took it up. However (in whatever manner) it came into composition, the effect was to freeze the traditional stream, making it viscous first, then solid and fixed. We may guess perhaps that here was a final stimulative effect before the scribes and the editors took over, and speech, the living voice, gave place to the text and the book came to the throne. The early books inherited the powers and organisation of the oral tradition. That is a large part of the explanation of their immense influence ever since, and of their miraculous massive pre-eminence. I am thinking not only of Homer and the Bible, but of the founding books of most of the great cultures. The *Analectus* and *Mencius* are good examples. They are the spoken word attributed suitably to Confucius or Mencius, written down later. I am not sure that the pre-eminence of Plato's earlier dialogues does not have the same explanation. Perhaps Socrates was wiser than he knew, in not writing. The point is that the new techniques of composition through writing, when super-imposed on the old techniques of speech, produced extraordinary results."

Extraordinary results. Not just results in a purely literary sense. Richards was primarily concerned with language and was analysing the shift from speech to writing from a literary point of view, though one could get glimpses of his concern for areas outside literature—philosophy, for instance, McLuhan, who went to Cambridge as a post-graduate student when Richards was already an established and respected don, sees this in a wider perspective:

"Until writing was invented, man lived in acoustic space:

> boundless, directionless, horizonless, in the dark of the mind, in the world of emotion, by primordial intuition, by terror. Speech is a social chart of this bog.
>
> "The goose-quill put an end to talk. It abolished mystery; it gave architecture and towns; it brought roads and armies, bureaucracy. It was the basic metaphor with which the cycle of civilisation began, the step from the dark into the light of the mind. The hand that filled the parchment page built a city."

McLuhan maintains that human experience is plural, a compound of many sensations, of sound, of sight, smell, taste, touch, mostly all at the same time, and its effective communication would depend on the medium that can transmit as much of all of these simultaneously. Sound, the maintains, is more effective in this process than sight. The spoken word activates us word can assert, stress, question, condemn, approve, with a force that the frozen written word cannot.

If the invention of writing brought about a minor revolution in communication, the invention of printing brought about a major one. "Printing," says McLuhan, "provided the first uniformly repeatable `commodity', the first assembly linemass production.

"It created the portable book, which men could read in privacy and in isolation from others. Man could now inspire—and conspire."

"Like easel painting, the printed book added much to the new cult of individualism. The private, fixed point of view became possible and literacy conferred the power of detachment, non-involvement."

But these transformations take time. Long sustained periods of literacy in a group's or nation's life would be necessary before perception by the eye supersedes 'aural' perception.

In his book, *Public Opinion in Russia*, Alexander Inkeles attributes to certain Soviet attitudes an unconscious bias which is rooted in their 'oral' perception of events. He says:

> "In the United States and England it is the freedom of expression, the right itself in the abstract, that is valued..... In the Soviet Union, on the other, the *results* of exercising freedom are in the forefront of attention, and the pre-occupation with the freedom itself is secondary. It is for this reason that the discussions between Soviet and Anglo-American representatives characteristically reach absolutely no agreement on specific proposals although both sides assert that there should be freedom of the press. The American is usually talking about freedom of *expression,* the right to say or not to say certain things, a right which he claims exists in the United States and not in the Soviet Union. The Soviet representative is usually talking about *access* to the *means* of expression, not the right to say things at all, and this access, he maintains, is denied to most in the United States and exists for most in the Soviet Union."

This is very close to their respective concepts of freedom. The removal of restrictions, the right to say what you want to say does not really constitute freedom, according to the Soviets. Freedom needs the creation of opportunities to exercise it. Otherwise it has no meaning. Freedom is a recognition of necessity. Whether the 'oral' society is at the root of it, I dare not say. But one does notice a distinct difference in the approach to propaganda of the western democracies and the Soviet Union. One stresses abstract values, rights; the other concrete gains, benefits. The one stresses the right of the individual, the virtues of free enterprise, of detachment, non involvement; the other, the good of the community as a whole and positive collective action to achieve it. And so on.

The point here we are trying to make is that it made the whole process of understanding (or misunderstanding) more complex. The pre-literate person listened with a different kind of concentration. Even many 'illiterate" communities of today do the same thing. The plural, the simultaneous sensations which the eloquent word created in us gave way to a kind of linear perception *via* the eye, of one word following the other. Our aids to memory took the form of diaries and notes and written instructions without which most of us are helpless—maps, time-tables, telephone directories, market prices, the stock exchange, newspaper headlines, street names, bill-boards. We have to remind ourselves and others that our thoughts have been put down on page so and so of our letter dated so and so in paragraph 3, line 4, and please note the words underlined. We have developed a lot of dodges to make ourselves understood— and not misunderstood when we use the written or the printed word. The written word, after all, is only a convenient device to put down our ideas. They can only give a rough idea of our thoughts. They can hardly indicate stress, cadence, rhythm, in spite of all the devices we have invented—commas upright or inverted; colons full or semi; stops full or partial; italics, parenthesis, dashes of all kinds; paragraphs, capitals, periods like in a music score in elaborate staff notation. We can put down everything reasonably accurately, clearly, to be studied and interpreted and understood. But the music is in the sound not on the score. Music reminds the Thirakwa, one of the great creative artists of our time, couldn't read or write as Akbar the Great couldn't. But at 94, he remembered clearly the *bols* he memorised as a boy, every syllable of it, and every syllable of every phrase he had learned since. And his stock of these is perhaps the biggest and greatest of any living tabla-player—an enormous repertoire in memory. He couldn't remember the names of his closest relatives, of streets, of the many places where he had lived and worked; not even of his many patrons and well-wishers. But the music he retained. Because he had to. It was a part of his life, of his very being, and he was a very different human being from his many pupils who wrote down and tried to memorise, if only a fraction of the knowledge he had to impart—not too satisfactorily. The Ustad's whole apparatus of music-making, of creativity, was different.

Musicians brought up in the Western tradition with the score playing a significant part in learning, in understanding, in performance, have a different approach to music than those brought up in an oral tradition like the Indian tradition. They remember passages as appearing on the top right hand corner of the page of a score. They hear the music by looking at the score, and what is more, they can see the score in front of their eyes while hearing the music. Most of them appreciate the music better if they can follow it with a score. I myself have no difficulty in judging an *alap* on a Sitar or a Veena with nothing but my ears, but to judge a piece of Western music, say, a string quartet, I would need a score. This is not merely the transference of an oral entity into a visual one, and the consequent inter-dependence of the two. This means different senses of perception, different stresses on values. How often do we hear the remark in the West, 'Not a particularly sensitive player, but a good sight-reader.' The ability to take in quickly with your eyes two or several more lines at one look, which is a gift of the eye, and the coordination of eye and hands, become an important part of the equipment of a musician. And music is purely an *aural* art. Sensitive creativity in music should surely not be left to good eyesights.

In *I was a Savage,* the autobiography of Prince Modupe, he tells us of an interesting incident. He had been to school and learned to read maps. He took home to his village a map of a river his father knew well and had used regularly as a trader, ".......my father thought the whole idea was absurd. He refused to identify the stream he had crossed at Bomako, where it is no deeper, he said, than a man is high, with the great widespread water of the vast Niger delta. Distances as measured in miles had no meaning for him....... Maps are liars, he told me briefly. From his tone of voice I could tell that I had offended him in some way not known to me at the time. The things that hurt one do not show on a map. The truth of a place is in the joy and the hurt that come from it. I had best not put my trust in anything as inadequate as a map, he counselled....... I understand now, although I did not at the time, that my airy and easy sweep of map-traced staggering distances, belittled the journeys he had measured on tired feet. With my big map-talk, I had effaced the magnitude of his cargo-laden, heat-weighted treks."

We don't often realise the changes that techniques of communication cause in social behaviour, in attitudes in general. A new technology in communication is not merely a new way of communicating thoughts, ideas, information. It creates a new way of life, a new kind of man. New techniques and inventions grow and catch on slowly, often unevenly. There was a long period of human history before writing was thought of; and there must have been a long period between the invention of writing and before it became anything remotely like a common heritage.

And of course there was the long break between writing and the invention of printing. Then suddenly in a matter of some 500 years or so after printing, Radio burst upon us, making communication possible on a mass basis. Two important links—the telegraph and wireless telegraph—in communication, the first signs of an electric medium entering the communication arena. The telegraph with its lines connecting one point to another became an accomplished and practical fact in the 1840s. Point to point communication with lines. This grew in quantity and complexity till cables were laid across the Atlantic (1858) and the sending of messages and information between Europe and any point in America became part of the communication scene. Then came wireless telegraphy. This is history now and even school-boys know the story of Marconi and his role in this. But let me, to keep up the continuity of the narrative, repeat it.

It was in 1896 that the British Association at its annual meeting made the public announcement of what was then described as 'space telegraphy'. The Chairman, Sir William Preece, stated that an Italian gentleman, called Guglialmo Marconi, had arrived in England with a 'magic' box which could send signals free of wires. There had been earlier hints of such phenomena when scientists had noticed sympathetic sparks and vibrations from unconnected sources, but Marconi is generally credited with the earliest realisation of the possibilities of wireless telegraphy.

Marconi, encouraged by Sir William, continued with his experiments and produced quick results. The Postmaster General also took a hand in this. In two years, exchange signals were sent across the channel. In another four years the distances had increased, and the signals were clear and strong enough to be used for Press News Services.

From then to the bridging of the Atlantic was only a logical step.

The wireless transmission of speech and music was a different matter and came later. It was Ambrose Fleming's invention of the thermionic two-electrode valve which made this possible and opened up a new world. A third electrode called the gird was added to this by Lee de Forest. The result was the triode valve, the key constituent of any broadcasting apparatus. The valve was soon developed and perfected to such an extent that clear, undistorted signals, whether of speech or music or drama, could be sent out to any part of the world and received satisfactorily. Hardly forty years had passed after the invention and the perfection of the valve before we found a substitute for it, smaller, more compact, cheaper; the ubiquitous transistor. But that is another story. Radio could present the world to the whole world. It made the dissemination of news, of information, of comment, of entertainment possible on a scale unprecedented in human history. The spoken word was rehabilitated with its full force—or nearly full force. And just as the supremacy of sound was being accepted as the key factor in communication, television overtook it; the visual element asserting itself again. All this in one's lifetime.

Until about a hundred and fifty years ago, the maximum speed at which a human being could travel was the speed of a horse. Just think of it. For two million years *homo sapiens* was held down to the speed of a horse and what is that? Thirty miles an hour? The stirrup was the best accelerator a rider had. But there was a limit to it. And then came the revolutionary discovery of the wheel. The whole concept of movement, of travel, of access, changed. The wheel led to the creation of the road, the road to settlements and so on and so on. The wheel also, of course, meant the potter's wheel—vast changes, developments in social attitudes and behaviour Eating vessels, drinking vessels, storage vessels, burial urns and what have you. Subtle artistry, delicate craft, form, balance. But let us stick to communication, of access from point to point.

The stirrup. The galloping horse. The message-carrying pigeon. The sailing ship. And all their minor and major variations. From that to the steam engine and the locomotive was an enormous step. The steam engine was not merely a faster mode of travel. Its range was fantastic. It could go non-stop, if you like from one end of the country to the other, whether it was a small country like England or a large country like the U.S.A. or Canada. The railway engine dıdn't tire like a horse. It could travel from one end of a continent to the other, right across and round the world at 30, 40, 50, 60, 80 or more miles an hour. The telegraph was perfected much about the same time as the locomotive—mid-nineteenth century. It was no accident that the telegraph poles dotted the railways lines and followed the same path. Both were products of the Industrial Revolution which itself was the culmination of the spirit of adventure, the questioning attitude, the emergence of the individual that the Renaissance and the Reformation initiated.

Remarkably, Renaissance and the Reformation had far-reaching effects on creativity and on social attitudes. First, a questioning attitude. Faith and Dogma were divested of their capital letters. Intuition and speculation gave way to reason and argument. The result? Moralities became drama—Marlowe, Shakespeare. Painting acquired a new dimension—perspective. Music developed tonality. Polyphony was on the scene. The new restlessness led to adventure, the conquest of the seas, the discovery of trade routes, of new lands to trade with. Expanding trade made the Industrial Revolution a necessity. In the rise and fall of civilisations, this was the age of Europe. Europe became the centre of the world, England really, because the British Empire was the biggest and most expansive of the various European empires. Greenwich set the time for the world. Parts of the world began to be named and known according to their proximity or relationship to Britain—the New World, the East or the West Indies, Middle East, Far East. East of what? Eat of London, of course. How can we in India, for instance, think of Iraq or Syria or Middle East when they are several hundred miles to the west of us? But we did as we were told, and called nations to the west of us as East. Things, of course, have changed since then.

The steam engine did a lot of things and was the crucial and central motive power for communications—trains of speed and comfort, trans-continental, international. Trains in which you could eat and sleep and cook and bathe, with bars and barber shops; ships which were floating luxury hotels with swimming pools and casinos and every known (some necessary and some quite unnecessary) aid to extravagance. And then quite suddenly came the internal combustion engine. As far as communications are concerned, the internal combustion engine meant the emergence of the automobile. From now on, the automobile takes over, slowly at first and then so rapidly, so pervasively, that in many parts of the world it has become part of a man's normal equipment. America started the car rush. The T-model Ford, a car that any lower middle-class man could buy for a month's or two month's income; and petrol, dirt cheap. By the middle of this century, every family in the United States had a car, some two, and a few even more. If the railway lines crisscrossed the country, the roads, dust-red at first, macadamised or concrete afterwards, rode and crossed in every direction reaching every nook and corner of the country, transforming thousands and thousands of square miles of green land into concrete slabs. They created a new type of life-line and a new type of lifestyle. Europe was not far behind and then Japan entered the race with a vengeance. The proud, magnificent looking railway engines began to the dethroned and the deluxe sleeping coaches with their handsome dining-rooms and executive suites began to vanish.

# 5

# Professional Organization of Mass Communicators

"When possible make the decision now, even if action is in the future. A reviewed decision usually is better than one reached at the last moment."

—*W.B. Given, Jr.*

In a preceding chapter, we have discussed the revolution in mass communication. The nature of the mass media has by now been established. Historically, it should be clear that through considerable economic growth the largest units are industrial-type businesses. As a result, although originally established for the intellectual task of purveying news and opinion, they have become factories geared for the mass production of advertising. They cater to public taste for information and entertainment primarily to get and hold a pool of regular readers, listeners, or viewers whose attention can be sold to advertisers. The news-gathering and reporting service, and the editorial or opinion pages, represent financially small parts of the whole.

Yet it is this news-reporting and opinion function upon which society relies for self-government. The news-reporting function has caused the press and government to be regarded as of coordinate importance; constitutional protection of the press against interference by government is grounded on the same reasoning. The reversal inside the firm in weight and scope of the information and the advertising roles brings about a confusion of the controls on accuracy and interpretation of the news. It is not the first instance of such confusion, but it is the first time that it has grown naturally out of a basic change in the economic structure of the media. It now appears that the self-righting process — that is, the provision for equal and open encounter between opposing points of view — is dependent upon the journalists' ability to assure a fair hearing for each of the important constituent groups in national and international society.

The control structure, as it supports or impedes the individual journalist's honesty, integrity, and courage in gathering, writing, and editing the news, and in expressing opinion, is similar to that affecting lawyers, doctors, and clergymen. It is impossible for a public agency to supervise the work of such individuals and unwise for it to attempt to do so. Journalists must check and correct each other, if it is to be done, and this means that they must construct and use a system of self-government based on professional ethics. The fact that they may be employed in a business primarily devoted to selling goods and services does not alter the lines of their responsibility, or those of business managers of the media, directly to society.

Can an ethical structure be provided within the individual business firm, and within the mass-communication industry, that will provide protection adequate to the needs of the community? To arrive at an answer to that question we must examine the control system already established and other contemporary ethical control structures in business and the professions, and venture a suggestion as to how the support needed by journalism could be constructed. We do not have a great deal of reliable information about the extent to which the public agrees or disagrees with the policy and the performance of the news media. Franklin D. Roosevelt's success over heavy opposition made it appear that the print media lack influence, but the long-term swing of popular voting from 1932 to 1956 is contrary.

Aside from their endorsement of political candidates, newspaper proprietors appear to hold few views or adhere to few policies in common. Efforts to study them have been frustrated by their somewhat canny reluctance to put their reputations in the hands of social-science research workers. However, we know from the Bernays surveys that some of the best of them, at least, believe the performance of the press varies from the ideals stated by respected figures in journalism.

**Staff Training and Discipline**

It is clear that deviations from ideal journalism arise in the control structure of the self-sufficient, closely-disciplined news room. As a group, journalists lack an image of themselves as persons of importance able to negotiate with the community from the strength of a set of assumptions that guarantees their security. They are under the kind of discipline, from the time of entering upon work as young men until they retire, that sharply limits their initiative; they are concerned about their personal performance and efficiency rather than the performance of the firm. In its simplest aspect, perhaps, this discipline has to do with the style of writing and the arbitrary choices that have to be made among words, word forms, abbreviations, kinds of sentence structure, and rigidly arbitrary headline forms. The journalist is accustomed to adjusting rapidly to the exigencies of available space and to the difficulties that the copyreader may confront in letter-counting a headline. But this authority over form, whether personalized or inherent in typographical limitations, is dogmatic and final; it engenders a frame of mind that makes it difficult to switch from obedience to dissent when discussion of policy takes place in the same context used to deal with grammar. In far too many offices this discipline is administered in schoolmasterish fashion by an editor who has arbitrary dismissal powers. As a result, the journalist develops a negative image of himself and his submissiveness increases.

Whether such powers are used (in some offices they are conditioned by labor contracts, in others by a professional spirit) is relatively less important than the psychological effect created when the journalist is subjected to rebuke and nagging in the intimate group to which his prestige is entrusted. The system of internal control is described by Warren Breed, a sociologist, who has studied non-metropolitan daily newspaper staffs. He limited himself to newspapers with 100,000 circulation or less, and thus excluded the largest and best-known newspapers in the country. However, the internal control system appears to be a function of the personality of the owner rather than size or metropolitan location.

*Formation of attitudes.* Editors, as a class senior to the journeyman journalist, form their attitudes during a considerable apprenticeship; they have been schooled in the publisher's policy while rising through the ranks. They read their own paper and become familiar with its social orientation. They have more or less frequent contact with the publisher through news conferences, policy meetings, routine office meetings, informal conversations, and perhaps social engagements. It is in the editor's own interest, in position, in advancement, and in enjoyment of the publisher's esteem, to know the office policy well. The editors do not take orders lying down. There is discussion, interaction, debate. The editor fights for his views, but it is taken for granted that the publisher has the final word when he wants it. This convention of discussion enables most editors to maintain their self-respect; few quit in disagreements with the publisher, and those who do tend to be younger men whose standards and values were brought in from the outside.

All in all, Breed says, the characteristics of the news operation, despite its association with the dynamic rush of events, are those of the slow-moving sacred society in which great emphasis is placed on harmonious protocol and obedience to authority. Writing what you know the boss wants to read is one road to recognition. "Nobody goes out and digs up something that is opposed to known policy." Breed says. "Thus the norms governing advancement in most cases are institutionalized in line with conformity." If a man shows independence in policy matters he is spoken to and set straight.

Policy, once formed, tends to perpetuate itself. It becomes part of the structure to be viewed as a value or norm. If it conflicts with reality, rationalizations are found to support policy rather than reality....News men retain various professional ideals but apparently the in-group norms and social relationships exert stronger pressure in the direction of policy.

*Behavioral patterns of journalists.* Breed classifies the staff men who have a relationship to executives on policy matters as follows: (1) Those who follow policy. (2) Those obligated to the boss for favors who therefore feel obligated to support his policy. Some staffs have a family spirit that accomplishes this purpose. (3) Those afraid to do anything except what they are told. (4) Those who follow because they respect the boss in spite of differences. (5) Open-minded writers of the sort who have not been disciplined to seek or ask for answers. Many such persons never think of professional obligations in terms of policy obligations. There is also an attitude of "Things are all right. Why fight?"

Staff members of this kind feel no responsibility to the public. They argue that it is hard to prove who is right, hard to find time to gather evidence to counter official opinion. In the absence of evidence, authority rules and staffers frequently exceed the policy demands of the office. (6) There are independent staff members who consistently write what they see and feel without regard to office policy, even though their copy is changed by an editor. Such reporters, Breed found, were fortunate in family background, have personal qualities preferred by the group, and are of high socio-economic status; often a tolerant publisher aids their independence; they have a clear picture of a newspaperman's professional obligations and a firm determination to live them. (7) Finally, there is the ethical reporter who quits his job in protest. Such a one usually is also disillusioned with the press as an institution. These are few, because even when a writer operates within policy restrictions he has some influence on what is printed and this salves his ego. He sees his job fundamentally as reporting, not as policy-making. Moreover, some of the reporters, because of personality differences, get more freedom than others and as a result the less fortunate ones personalize their feelings of frustration. This diverts their attention from the boss. Because he is satisfied with his work, the newsman is not alert to the shortcomings of his vocation. Stereotypes and traditional ways of doing things more readily perpetuate themselves when critical appraisal is lacking. Routine is his great enemy. Journalists are not rewarded for conceptualizing or analyzing social problems, but for being reporters and editors satisfactory to management.

News is a never-ending stream, a continuous challenge, and meeting the daily challenge is the newsman's job. In this process news becomes a value to the newsman. It guides his activity in important ways. He defines situations in terms of news values, acts and reacts in terms of them.... The true professional man probes into his motives; he is fully acquainted with the elements of his work..... Until [the journalist's] awareness of societal inter-relationships is increased, probably by better training, his work will be hampered by standardization and tradition rather than fixed by a systematic professional group.

**Professionalism Principles**

The system of discipline for newsgatherers or reporters is not professional because most of the journalists do not take part positively in creating the spirit of the establishment. Instead, they are persuaded by the same routine of training and indoctrination that could produce a truly professional spirit to accept the role and the discipline that goes with the status of hired man. The question that now arises is whether or not this role for the journalist is the one that serves the best interests of the community and, if not, what changes might be suggested in the public interest? This question is cardinal and fundamental: it brings into examination long-standing concepts of the role of the proprietor, the manager, and the employee. There is no standardized role for management, however.

The power to hire and fire confers, by itself, no particular insight or skill in the management of men, and business history records an infinite variety of experimentation.

Professionalism is simply one of the ways of seeking out the best employees available and of using the following principles, among others, in working with them:

1. Management is only as intelligent as its employees and co-workers; all things considered, the most intelligent employee requires direction only in the sense of utilizing his drive, giving it, along with the energy of co-workers, unified purpose and a sense of direction.
2. A man who is interested in his work will give better service than one who is one. He comes to identify himself with the firm and to feel he has a stake in it; he will require less supervision, produce more work, of higher quality, and provide a better example for others, than an employee who lacks such identification.
3. Orderly classification of jobs and personnel policies — pay, promotion, problem and policy consultation, grievances — is part of the minimum professional system. This system curbs and harnesses many of the critical aspects of rivalry between men and assures the firm a level of experience and education suitable to each position.
4. Staff direction is supported by a consultation system based on order and precedent and is relatively free of whim and caprice.
5. Opportunities are provided for employees to get further education and to develop special competence that carries prestige with readers and fellow workers.

6. Opportunities are provided for leading members of the staff to cover news events of first importance wherever they happen, to become regional or national as well as local authorities on special problems.
7. Salary schedules compare favorably with community and national averages for work of similar difficulty and, in any event, are high enough to keep the salary negotiations of the professional-class employees out of the trade-union pattern.
8. All the news of importance is printed or broadcast without deferring to the selfish interests that may be affected.
9. Pension rights are funded and accompany the man if he changes jobs.
10. Financial control is unaffected; management retains all initiative and veto rights, but it is committed to delegating as much as possible of staff direction and work processes to professional-class employees. If delegation is incomplete, the benefits are reduced or denied; if delegation goes too far, if the authority is no longer actively and firmly in the hands of participant owners, the incentives are diluted and the staff may lack competition and drive.

In fact, in system is not simple to install and maintain, but when carefully managed it produces an institution that will maximize return on capital over the long run. It gives the owners the pleasure of association with intellectual equals and true companions and saves both the loneliness and frustration of running a business solely by giving orders to one or two associates.

There are two general concepts of professional

organization of the press. The one most widely explored assumes that the ethics of journalism and of business are in conflict and that journalists must organize to protect themselves against the spirit of the counting room. This concept dominated the testimony of working journalists presented to the Royal Commission on the Press in England. Witnesses complained that the editor had lost status and power and that the business manager had taken over his prerogative. It is also implicit in the Hutchins Commission's report wherein the press is told to provide the improved service society needs or risk governmental interference.

The other concept is that the whole institution, business and communication combined, should undertake professionalization. Although less often found in scholarly consideration, this concept accepts the unity of communicators and their business partners, rather than seeking to make them opponents within the same firm. The whole-institution proposal offers the best opportunity for long-run success. It is the only kind of professionalism we have at this time.

The omission of government from any part in the relationship is deliberate, and eliminates any possibility that professionalism would be considered an abridgement of freedom of the press. The press is by now familiar with the ability of government to modify policies within a firm or an industry with reference to advertising, manufacturing, or distribution. In all respects except in the standards of writing and editing, the mass media have long been regulated in the public interest. Management, for example, is left free to fix wages above a certain minimum, subject to its ability to bring in revenues to meet the costs. The standards of advertising copy are regulated by law, by shop and community rules enforced by management, and by a large number of state and federal boards, including the Federal Trade Commission, the Food and Drug Administration, and the Post Office Department.

All of the regulatory measures, private and official, have been adopted in response to sustained public criticism of business hardly different from the criticism of political bias in the news which is currently heard.

## Editors and Managers as Rivals

Is the counting room a place which by its very nature excludes ethics of the sort needed by journalism? Is it hopeless to think of professionalizing the business of journalism and should attention be given, therefore, only to reporters and editors? An answer might depend upon the extent to which the professional ideals stated above are supported by conventions existing in business. Would journalists organized apart from businessmen in the same institution be competent to define and meet the responsibilities outlined for them herein? That would depend on whether they were willing to accept a goal much more limited than that of the whole-institution concept. Their control would be, in the main, negative, even though it might have a number of positive benefits to society.

The creative leadership needed to expand the information report would remain in the businessmen who handle the purse.

## A Radical Program of Reform

Haydn Davies, one of the journalist members of Parliament who testified before the Royal Commission, asked for legislation which would prevent owners from controlling their own businesses. He suggested outlawing monopolies, a statutory press commission treating the press as a public utility, fixed ratios of advertising and news, fixed prices, elimination of all sales promotion except that calling attention to intrinsic values of the publication, and tax relief for proprietors who, in effect, would turn their stock interest and dividends over to a foundation. Finally, he wanted the government to own all printing facilities and to lease them to those who wish to print periodicals. No newspaper could be sold or its doors closed without government consent. Mr. Davies' ideas show the massive controls that would be necessary to separate the editorial and business departments of a communication medium. They did not find approval inside the Royal Commission or elsewhere in the non-socialist world. They are in part quite like the ideas used by the post-World War II Czechoslovak government in its "bright passage" phase from a syndicate-type democracy to Communism. Even so, ideas of this sort deserve examination of their origins and purposes. If the origin is in frustration, meaning that such proposals are the products of fruitless attempts by minority parties to get a hearing for political alternatives in an open society, they do not deserve to be ignored. Restraint of trade in political ideas, no matter how high-minded and patriotic the monopolists, means—in the parlance of the market—bankruptcy for democracy. The newspaper proprietor, as the man who has the strongest motive to manage his own capital, is inseparable from the mass-communications establishment in capitalistic society, and there is more point in considering a code of professional bahavior for the whole establishment than one solely for news personnel. A balance of ideas in the market place of thought requires concern with the whole establishment. A code limited to the editorial department would either be weakly effective or result in a shift of responsibility to men without training for the job.

Does the moral web of the community support business principles upon which a professional organization of the press may be built? Are the principles enunciated by Clarence Francis adequate? Are they able to get acceptance as building blocks in a professional structure? Business provides a basis for an ethical system more representative of society than does the craft of the journalist. Businessmen are accustomed to think about and deal practically with community-wide problems. The leaders among them have come to accept responsibility for the economic progress of the community, as defined both by themselves and by governmental policy, and insofar as that progress may be realized by initiative, intelligence, and work. In spite of the number of narrow persons among them, a narrow view of community objectives does not prevail, and present goals are subject to enlargement by discussion.

Journalists, by occupation, are trained for a passive but intellectual role in the service of the community and its leadership groups. Not all journalists accept this role; many admire and would follow the example of Greeley in his effort to organize the community politically as well as to lead it intellectually; but when they move out of the editorial conference room into the theater of political action, they no longer are subject to the authoritative interaction of other journalists alone but to the authority of the political group which they have joined.

Businessmen grow up in roughly the same ethical environment as journalists, but today the responsibilities of business include the progress of the community, higher standards of living, higher productivity and abundance, control of the swings of the business cycle, as well as keeping the community favorable to the market place. Businessmen may lead or at least support such large-scale adjustments as the flight to the suburbs, but some of them — particularly those still in the central city — will also be interested in clearing away the blighted areas left behind; when curative measures are taken, businessmen will do the work. They are interested in freedom, although they are not always aware of the reciprocal obligations that attach to it and some may not voluntarily accept the rights-and-duties convention, but in this they are by no means alone; they are selfishly interested in maintaining freedom of choice, to avoid having their hands tied by regulations.

They occupy the central position in the communications institutions and they, and only they, have at this time the capacity to evoke a professional spirit in their establishments and to dedicate it to the community. They have at their disposal the bulk of the imagination, leadership, and enterprise needed, and they have control of the resources available for the work. Businessmen are increasingly aware, because of studies they accept, of the extent to which the individual, in J.M. Clark's words, is "molded in body, mind, and character by his economic activities and relations, stimuli and disabilities, freedoms and servitudes" so that he is the social product of the system he helps maintain.

In addition, a surprisingly large number of businessmen—surprising in view of the prevailingly unfavorable publicity business has received at the hands of historians and social scientists in general — have high standards of truthfulness in advertising and selling, fair competition, fair self-assessment and payment of taxes and what Bowen calls the "rules of the game" of business.

The concern that business has for the economic well-being of the community might be described as enlightened self-interest, the kind of practical ethics that businessmen were taught in the nineteenth century. A moral judgment in this setting was likely to be motivated by religious teaching, internalized in conscience. In its post- depression twentieth-century orientation, the Judeo-Christian import of ethics has shifted away from the individual conscience to a pragmatic evaluation of action in terms of the risk that it will trigger legislative restraints or other reprisals by the community. Bowen says that the nineteenth-century ethical heritage of business influences men to (1) observe the rules of property; (2) honor contracts; (3) refrain from deception and fraud; (4) be efficient and promote economic progress; (5) protect life and limb and the health of workers and the general public; (6) compete vigorously and, in case of the failure of competition, to act with restraint; (7) accept and respect the economic freedom of consumers, workers, and owners; and (8) have regard for the human rights of workers. These rules were implicit in Adam Smith's economic theory as contained in *The Wealth of Nations,* because his concept united self-interest and the public interest. That these goals were somewhat beyond the ordinary reach of men, as are some of those expressed by Clarence Francis, does not invalidate the claim that they influence conduct. When A.T. Stewart, the New York large-scale merchant, established a policy of one price for all, plainly marked, and granted reasonable return privileges to his customers, he was applying literally the moral code of the nineteenth as well as the twentieth century, and the fact that his policies received considerable publicity and were widely copied by others, including Wana-maker, shows that in them the practical blending of ethics and business policy had a certain evangelical character in its impact on the public.

Bowen says it has been the lot of businessmen since the enormous growth of industry that they have been judged as ethically derelict when in reality their problems stemmed more from malfunctioning of the economic system than from the ethical system. Large-scale enterprise conferred a power on individual capitalists derived from monopoly or concentration; fluctuations in business activity beyond the control of businessmen in a free-enterprise system produced unemployment and dislocation of human beings; technological unemployment grew out of the need to conserve resources and increase productivity; society afforded inadequate protection against illness and old age; the disparities in income and opportunity made the lot of some men intolerable and the life of others bare and uninteresting; there was wasteful exploitation of natural resources when the community lacked the wisdom or legal apparatus to protect itself. Some men were degraded by materialistic, competitive, and invidious standards of consumption.

And there was frequent disregard for the social costs of economic activity. The present-day mixed economy, the blend of freedom and regulation, resulted from social legislation critical of business operations. This criticism tended to express the ethical norms of the community; business practices were emended and today reflect an entirely different relationship to stockholders and to the community than in the nineteenth century. Observance of the reaction of business to public opinion since the great depression provides hope for the objectives implicit in this concept. Although the ultra-conservative elements, those obviously favoring a system of business tyranny, have become more clearly visible as a result of heavy taxation and controversial legislation meshing american economic interests with those of other countries, the liberal element has also become more visible and effective. The intensity of conflict within the community provides an index of the responsiveness of some businessmen to the demands of public opinion and the reluctance of others to accept a new interpretation of self-interest in terms of public interest.

The reaction of business to public opinion also suggests that improvement of ethical attitudes will flow from more clearly articulated public demand. The communications media, being at the center of and visible to the whole community, cannot escape the full impact of this demand. Businessmen are members of society who have acquired many or most of the social expectations of what business should contribute to the community.

The wide diffusion of ownership has given greater influence to professional managers who sit as members of a council on policy and project today's problems into the future, correcting insofar as they can for trends that appear unfavorable. "Business is sensitive to changes in the market for its goods and equally sensitive to changes in the market for the business system itself. In both markets it will rise to what is expected of it — but not much higher than that," Bowen says. When professionalization of journalism is considered, it is often said that journalism does not fully possess either the general or the legal-medical criteria and it is sometimes assumed that for it professionalization is therefore difficult if not impossible. Such a conclusion overlooks the infinite variety professionalism takes; moreover, the practice of law and medicine is undergoing changes which bring it constantly closer to the institutional forms of journalism.

The Hutchins Commission, observing that most journalists are employees and that their employers take ultimate responsibility, found little hope that journalism could reach professional status. It observed: No public service is more important than the service of communications. But the element of personal responsibility, which is of the essence of the organization of such professions as law and medicine, is missing in communications. Here the writer works for an employer, and the employer, not the writer, takes the responsibility. In the mass media, except at the higher levels of writing, the identity of the individual writer's product tends to be merged in a joint result, as in newspapers, where it is divided among reporter, copy desk, and makeup desk. The effective organization of writers on professional lines is therefore almost impossible. The techniques used by journalism are, indeed, the same techniques used by literate and scholarly men throughout the ages; to them have been added the facilities of printing and these expand the responsibility of the journalist through the community in somewhat the same way that the responsibilities of teachers and ministers are spread through the community. Edition deadlines require completion of work in a fixed time, seriously straining the ability of the journalist to go through the routine of verification and evaluation of material which scholars prize so highly. Ability to do reliable work under these conditions results from mastery of specialized techniques. Do these techniques, even assuming their special difficulty, deserve classification as of less than professional grade merely because many men are literate and could do the work of journalists if they had extra training in work at high speed and under pressure? The answer appears to be affirmative unless the techniques and adaptation result from and are accompanied by a long period of systematic training that clearly makes the journalist a specialist, possessing not only the general arts of literacy but specific understanding that non-journalists do not have.

The method by which newsmen are paid differs little from the way many doctors and lawyers in corporate or group practice are paid, but the range of earnings finds journalists in an inferior position and this fact causes many of them, at the peak of their abilities, to leave journalism for public relations or some other work. At the same time, others equally competent stay on all their lives.

Though journalists have a sense of responsibility for the competence and honor of the profession as a whole, they are frustrated in making this concern felt because there is no public or private forum in which they are free to express themselves. The lawyer and doctor are put under obligation to identify and to adopt the best available techniques. There is a large and complex system of professional publications serving, through reports of research, to criticize and rectify imperfect procedures and practices that do not meet professional standards. The journalist who wishes to identify the best techniques and to assert leadership must create his own forum, provide his own publication, and distribute it. If he has charges to bring against an unethical colleague, he must act in a situation where the values are more those of supervised schoolboys than of a mature profession. Now we come to responsibility of the joint product.

As to the assertion that the journalist's product tends to be merged in a joint result by the overlapping authority of the writer, the copy editor, and the makeup desk, there is hardly an essential difference in the organization of responsibility here than in the operating room of a hospital. If anything goes wrong with the way a story is handled it is fairly easy to pinpoint the blame; the law holds both author and publisher responsible. The task of the original writer is very complex: he deals with a living system in which his powers of observation are subject to several kinds of error. He is judged and criticized according to his ability to present a clear, concise, meaningful, and objective account of a significant event or phenomenon.

After the story is written it has the stability of inert matter; it is not very hard to tell who did what in the editing and printing processes. It is more difficult to decide whose judgment was correct, but this is also true of a surgical team operating with a complex, living subject capable of several kinds of spontaneous reaction. The group practice of law is also a fixture of the complex society.

The lawyer is often as much responsible to the other lawyers for his performance as is the journalist to others of his staff, and while somebody in the firm is ultimately responsible to the client, the lawyer has at stake his public reputation—normally of greater value to him than an individual fee. The journalist is less firmly rooted in one community only because his relationship to other journalists is governed by the rules of business rather than by the conventions of a profession. This impairment of journalistic status is not difficult to remedy, for it can be corrected by a more intense educational experience and by conventions inside the firm which confer commensurate status and dignity on the journalists. How Professionalism Comes About. The impetus for a professional movement can develop either within or without the vocation concerned. If it arises within, the motive may be partly to create a shelter of monopoly under which practitioners can pursue their self-interest and partly to improve services to the community. If it arises without, it comes usually when society is in an ugly mood of reaction against abuses inside the vocation.

Such an ominous and emotional mood is likely to result in blunderbuss efforts at correcting abuses through legislation; the only countermeasure open to practitioners is to correct or prevent abuses themselves. When there is no professional organization, when as a consequence the practitioners are apathetic toward community needs, the way is open for non-moral behavior, for corruption and abuse of the institution. In the media, apathy forces the best elements to provide a shield behind which the incompetent elements can work their will in their communities. Freedom of the press, they say, protects them in their apathy, and it does.

When professional controls exist in a democratic society they tend to be highly decentralized. This makes them more difficult to use, and if they are not used a condition of disgust even worse than apathy develops as practitioners react against the pseudo-professionalism from which they had expected so much. A professional system without significant standards of excellence and discipline is worse than unorganized status, for society is likely to relax its vigilance, at least for a time, when professional controls are established. Professional organization is not effective without high-quality leadership, but it does provide rewards and recognition for leaders; in fact, professional organization is useless unless it is clearly an expression of an already existing professional spirit. Although this spirit may be shared by a minority of the persons affected, when it exists in a valid setting it can be taught to others.

The importance of journalism is that it is a communications vehicle for leadership of all sorts in the community, a vehicle provided either by its practitioners in their own right or by them in their capacity as transmission agents for other leaders. Mass communication has a virtual monopoly on the attention of the mass public. If society is to be efficiently organized it would seem that the press will have to take part either as a principal or as an agent of principals. Apathy of individuals with respect to the whole society under these circumstances entails assignment of the leadership role on the basis of random or accidental factors and each crisis arising in the community makes necessary the selection of new leaders and the building of a new organization to deal with it.

*Feedback from the community.* Professional organization and communication provide the feedback of signals which enables individuals and firms to monitor their behavior. In the long run, the use of such feedback by an elite inside the professional group appears to be the only substitute for control from the outside by untrained members of the general public. It is feedback that provides an opportunity for a firm or practitioner to relate activities to social norms. Otherwise, events in the outside world appear to have no relevance; one can do as he pleases. For the firm, this feedback may have implications for news or editorial policy, for attitudes of employees toward the public, or for some aspect of service relationships with the public. For the individual, it may have to do with adequate training for the role of journalist, performance in an instance important to the community, conflicts or agreement between personal or professional behavior and the social norm. At any rate, it is clear that instilling moral norms in the individual is not sufficient guarantee of professional behavior in the social interest; the situation of society is so complex that a set of institutional principles is needed to which the individual practitioner can refer when he is confronted with circumstances for which there is no norm, or at least none known to him. Professionalism provides these principles and specific rules as interpreted in the long stream of interaction with the community: it helps reject apathy and drift as directing forces in the organization of society.

*Tests for entering a profession.* Professional men give expression to their sense of responsibility by providing tests for the entrance of neophytes. Professional organizations in law and medicine, working with schools to which they can give or withhold accreditation — that is, the right to operate inside the profession — prescribe a minimum course of study for all trainees and cap this with formal examination and the issuance of a revocable license to practice. Many other professional organizations, including those of public-school teaching, social welfare, accounting, public administration, engineering, and architecture, also establish effective minimum standards in one way or another. At present, the only generally applied tests for entrance to the practice of journalism are the ability to read and write, and some critics of journalism doubt that this test is administered so as to catch all illiterates.

The joint interests and responsibilities of the firm with respect to advertisers and readers must be acknowledged, but they are clearly separable. Insofar as the entrepreneur in mass communication employs his capital for the sale and distribution of advertising services, the courts have held that he has no special privileges in business or in society. But in his semi-industrial role as a collector and disseminator of information, he has considerable protection against interference, because it is assumed that the political system cannot survive without this service. If adversaries conspire to use personal or political power to threaten his income from advertising in order to weaken his independence as a carrier of information and opinion, government will protect his establishment if called upon to do so. But if he chooses to give in to pressure rather than ask for protection, and if he surrenders quietly without the public's knowledge, the information he purveys is biased and works to accomplish a distortion of the political system. The protection society affords the press against official intimidation is considerable: it includes habeas corpus, trial by jury, sharp limitations upon the contempt powers of the courts, protection against special and punitive legislation, and a flat ban on the censorship of political material. But the private pressures on the management of mass-communication enterprises work against no countervailing force except that which is capable of ethical description. Only the personal character and intelligence of the individual entrepreneur, as expressed in his own actions and in instructions to his staff, protects the public against pollution of its information sources. And if the contaminants are carefully apportioned so as not to cause widespread loss of confidence, the mixture can be continued indefinitely. Typically, it is the work of ethical organization to monitor institutional performance in reporting news and to implement counterpressures to apathy and corruption. To say that advertising is in a position to dominate the mass media of communication is by no means correct, for, if in the mind of the controlling entrepreneur, his role in providing public information is of greater value than the service he performs for advertisers, regardless of the relative size of his income from readers and from merchants, then advertising merely contributes to support of the economic facility by which the news is carried to the masses in a manner and on a scale befitting the industrial age. It does not exert a damaging influence on contents of a medium whose staff is determined to put the news value first.

### The Professional Council of the Press

The importance of a professional council has been mentioned. A council can give wide support to professional standards. The British, with a press system almost identical to ours, introduced a General Council of the Press for this purpose in 1953. It is an independent body of twenty-five members supported by organizations of editors, journalists, and newspaper proprietors; its jurisdiction is national in scope.

Fifteen members represent editors and journalists and ten represent owners. The participating groups are the British Guild of Newspaper Editors, somewhat like the American Society of Newspaper Editors; the National Union of Journalists, comparable to the American Newspaper Guild; the Institute of Journalists, an organization with some of the characteristics of Sigma Delta Chi, the ASNE and the Guild; the Newspaper Society, composed of proprietors of provincial dailies and London and provincial weeklies, a group somewhat like an amalgam of the regional daily groups, Inland Daily Press Association, Southern Newspaper Publishers Association, and the National Editorial Association; and two Scottish groups of proprietors. The members are elected by the groups they represent for three-year terms.

The purposes of the British Council, as set out in its constitution, are to defend the established freedom of the press, to maintain the highest professional and commercial standards, to keep under review problems of access to information, to aid education for journalism, to "promote a proper functional relation among all sections of the profession," to promote research, to study concentration and monopoly, and to publish reports of its work and its investigations.

*What the Council does.* In practice, the Council sits to consider any problems it finds to be within its stated objects and it receives communications from the public and from government officials about the performance of the press. It has a general-purposes committee which meets on call and which investigates complaints about press performance. The full Council holds quarterly meetings, issuing statements of its findings after each meetıng that are widely quoted in the press. It also publishes an annual report. Its sole method of influencing either the press or the public is through the medium of its public statements. These have the character, though not the force, of court opinions and are based on investigation and consideration of the facts in disputes brought to its attention. The Council has no privilege against libel suits or contempt action by the courts or Parliament; it is under the same obligation as any journalistic group to issue accurate reports.

*Criticism of Journalistic Behavior.* The largest part of the Council's business is dealing with complaints about the behavior of journalists in line of duty — complaints alleging violations of privacy; imposition on persons in the news or their families; sensationalism and even pornography in news, features, and photographs; breaches of professional ethics; and infringements of official privilege by publication of restricted documents. The Council has found itself speaking for the press in explaining how journalism does it work and what freedom of the press consists of. It has defended the popular mass-circulation newspapers except as to exploitation of sex crimes and sensation in the news and has been attacked, on this account, as a gang of journalists defending other journalists. To such complaints the Council has replied simply that it does not defend journalists, but the freedom of the press.

The problems dealt with are those which have long caused tension between the press and the public. Before the establishment of the Press Council complaints about press performance rarely were answered; the public tended to build up a general attitude of ire and indignation against the press. Prompt investigation by the Press Council has helped to clear away some of the indignation, but has not satisfied everyone. The Council says that some of the critics are "in need of the curbs they propose for others, since they themselves are guilty of the offenses they allege — wild exaggeration, distortion of the truth, and the unproved assumption that they speak for the nation." It has not hesitated to censure particular newspapers and particular journalists when they are found guilty of unprofessional practices. The Council's statements have been widely published, thus giving publicity to a wide variety of case studies of journalistic standards. They have made it more difficult for editors and journalists to engage in unethical and unfair competitive practices. When journalists have been unjustly accused, or have been imposed upon by persons selfishly interested in getting into print only their own version of an event, the Press Council has defended them with dignity and firmness.

*Criticism of the Council.* Thus the Council considers disputes according to the established ethical system of the community and lets its decision run accordingly. When criticized as ineffectual, it replies that it does not want the legal power to summon witnesses and take testimony under oath, nor the power to disqualify or punish journalists found guilty of unprofessional practices. Such powers would bring in the government and might interfere with freedom of the press, it says. Many critics find the Council unsatisfactory because it consists solely of journalists and is weakly financed by its sponsors. These critics describe reproof of erring journalists as mere slaps on calloused wrists. All such criticism runs either to the admitted immaturity of professional spirit or to the demand that the Council take on official status. The proponents of an official Council have yet to demonstrate that it is compatible with political freedom.

# 6

# Audio-Visual Revolution

"I think the first virtue is to restrain the tongue: he approaches nearest to the Gods, who knows how to be silent, even though he is in the right."

—*Cato*

Advancement in science and technology has changed the face of all human activities. Mass Media and mass communication are not untouched with it. Rather a great revolution came in this field particularly after coming of recent ICT.

Here in this chapter we have touched the Audio-visual communication. Though as of now, say in 2009 many new things have come making older obsolete.

## Visual Communication

A visual aid is any visible device that assists an instructor to transmit to a learner facts, skills, understanding, knowledge and appreciation. The visual method is actually an aid to use with other methods of instruction, rather than a method in itself. It is particularly useful with the dramatisation and lecture method. In the visual method, instruction is carried on through such devices as film strips, slides, movies, photographs, charts, posters, cartoons, models and actual objects. It is used as far as possible, as visual sense, is measured as effective as an avenue of learning. The visual sense can be increased to a great extent by visual aids. Quick and past presentation can be achieved which show a relationship among ideas, facts and can serve as a review device. The aids should be clear, simple, legible, interesting to have positive effect. It is practically possible to use visual media in combination of other media.

Facts, figures etc., can be presented in an early assimilable manner so that information can be spelled out exactly and the same helps to picturise the required matter. In corporate organisation the executives can substantiate the policies and the goals of the corporation with reference to data properly presented by the pictures. Like other electronic media, visual media also play a significant role in bringing up the communication gap. Here one should remember the recently developed technology, namely, audio-visual. In this technique visual technology is the key factor as a tool to give effect to audio-visual communication. Visual device is an aid to audio and audio is just an aid to visual communication that implies opinions, expression, interpretation, explanation and narration of the pictures, photos, slides, etc.

Visual aids alone cannot make the communication adequate by itself. To be effective it must be supported by interpretation and narration by the transmitter. In communication visual aid helps observation. It is also an effective means of communication and developed techniques widely practised by the business and industrial houses, educational institutions, meetings, conferences etc. It can be used to communicate the communicator's thoughts and ideas through a visual medium. Presentation of figures, statistical data can effectively be presented through visual aid. Visual aids represent a message by symbols. Using visual aids is combined with oral message with a view to clarify, explain to convince and even to attract the listeners' attention or interest. A number of factors are responsible to the receptive to visual aids.

**Types of Visual Aids**

There are many kinds of visual aids. They include such devices as tables, charts, graphs, photographs, maps, diagrams, pictorial presentation, visual projection, cine, the slide, overhead projectors etc. All kinds may not be useful for all kinds of messages. It is the responsibility of the efficient communicator to exercise his skill in the selection of appropriate visual aids. As a matter of fact choice of suitable visual material depends on several factors such as:

(1) The need and requirements of the organisation.

(2) The nature of subject matter to be transmitted.

(3) The group of people or listeners to whom the subject matter of message is intended to put across.

(4) The selection of appropriate aid among various kinds of visual materials available to meet the purpose.

(5) The object of transmitting a particular piece of message.

(6) The attitude and the capabilities of the listeners to observe visual aid and understand the message.

(7) The nature of the message to be presented in the aid.

(8) The availability of adequate expert people to prepare aids.

(9) The time, cost and labour factors also to be considered.

(10) Any special purpose for which visual method is to be adopted.

(11) The knowledge of the transmitter as to how it is to be operated.

There are various types of charts such as lines, bars, mathematical graphs, pictograms, cartograms, diagrams, areagraphs, bargraphs, grouped bar, subdivided bar, range bar, step bar, twin bar, gantt chart, paired bar, deviation bar, sliding bar, column bar, histogram, curvegraph, slice graph, matrics graph, multi-scale graph, cumulative graph, cumulative frequency graph or ogive index graph, z chart, frequency polygon, semi-log graph, log graph, band graph, etc.

*1. Overhead Projector.* Overhead projector is one of the most advanced and efficient visual aid. By tilting lens head up and, down and adjusting levelling legs, it is possible to produce uniform pictures. The machines has light equalising reflector, light intensifying condenser etc., which gives consistently bright and sharp picture.

*2. Charts, Graphs etc.:* A chart is a pictorial presentation in the form of a table or diagram of information about a particular subject. Chart depicts non-numerical relationship and a graph depicts quantitative relationship. Information may be presented by charts, graphs etc. They are by far the most used visual aids. May be painted, printed or drawn.

*3. Flannel Board:* The ordinary meaning of the word implies a piece of matcrial made of cotton or wool. A cotton cloth made in imitation of flannel. Flannel boards consist of a board covered with felt. Sticky backed visuals are placed on surface. It allows the speaker to put some action or movement and flexibility into an otherwise static presentation.

*4. Fascimile:* Facsimile is a mechanical media makes an exact copy. Fascimile transmits through telephone lines, exact copies of blue prints, layouts and other visual materials. It is increasingly used to transmit exact copies between distant places. So it is used popularly to send copies between an organisation and communication medium or between the offices of agency and client.

*5. Magnetic Boards:* Magnets permit the use of heavier three dimensional visuals. Magnetic boards are similar like flannel boards. The only special feature with magnetic boards is that magnets permit the use of heavier three dimensional visuals.

*6. Electro-writers:* Writing caused by electricity. Electro writers are generally used by the executives or demonstrators. They can write their black board notes through a long distance through a transmitter unit hooked up by telephone lines with projector unit and screen.

*7. Telelectures:* Telelecture as a visual aid has been discussed elsewhere in detail. It is a common tool for making an audio/visual presentation at a distance. A best technique for making audio/visual presentation at distance. With the arrangement of telephone department there is hook up from a speakers office to a meeting place or class room or conference where visuals can be shown while speaker is heard.

*8. Audio and Video Cassettes etc.:* A number of electronic media have emerged in the field of communication. They are highly sophisticated communication technologies produced by devices made according to the principles of electronics. There are a number of electronic media available and is gaining importance all over the world. They are likely to revolutionise communication system. To mention they are video cassettes, audio cassettes, video disc, telidon, video tape, videotex, disc recording etc. They are useful in overcoming some of the difficulties associated with conventional media.

**Guidelines for Using Visual Aids**

(1) The media should enrich or increase the listener's, viewer's knowledge as a basis for decision-making.

(2) They must show the most important and significant matters referred in the oral discussion part.

(3) To prepare charts, diagrams or transparent paper typed before beginning speech.

(4) Pictures, slides etc., should be attractive and interesting.

(5) They should clearly and precisely clarify or explain a point or to convince and at the same time to attract the attention or interest of the observer at a glance.

(6) Keep the aids in the order and sequence in which oral part of the text follows.

(7) Each aid should bear a caption or label clearly and lucidly.

(8) The observer capable of being to grasp the pictorial message quickly and correctly.

(9) The captions or titles or labels should be as far as possible in capital letters or written in bold letters. This will help not only the people who are farthest

away but also can be read and understood at a glance.

(10) Avoid all distraction activities in the place of display.

(11) Display visual aids with sufficient light or in a dark room depending upon the type of aid used.

(12) Select appropriate time and context of text discussion to show aids.

(13) Wherever necessary footnote explanation, should be given at the end of or at the bottom of picture or chart.

(14) Visual aids should be simple and good enough to depict the message to help the observer to comprehend quickly.

(15) It is desirable to use different colours to draw attention to a particular aid.

(16) Accuracy of message incorporated in the aids and which need to be matched with the spoken words is atmost important for smooth transition and discussion.

**Major Advantages**

It is remarkable to note that the visual media are more extremely useful. The advantages of visual media can be enumerated as below.

*1. Quick Communication:* Visual aids are known for quicker communication. Speedy communication is necessary in respect of certain subject matters. Where certain important facts or figures need to be highlighted or attractive observation is necessary, the visual aids are more useful.

*2. Understanding at a Glance:* Visual techniques like pictures, slides etc., enable the observer to concentrate on them to understand at a glance. This merit is not available in respect of other oral and written communication.

*3. Comparison:* Charts and graphs depicting data for various years so that they facilitate easy comparison of data by observing trend line having characters of constant or up and down movement. The figurative relationship can be presented pictorially.

*4. Memorising Effect:* Message in a pictorial form may long last in the mind. The observers can carry home on a permanent way and recall and refresh the image whenever he wants. It has more memorising effect. A well designed aid can project a distinctive image of the situation and hence more memorable.

*5. Bird's Eyeview:* Charts, graphs, slides and other visual aids give a bird's eyeview of a given text of subject matter shown at appropriate time and spot. The information presented on them is easily understood, simple, readily comprehensible and intelligible.

*6. Dynamic:* Information transmission is a continuous process, routine on different matters. So the subject matter of communication may continuously be changing based on activities, work and correspondence. Visual aids can be prepared accordingly to changing needs. Therefore, visual aids are not static but dynamic. They carry greater force through its ability to demonstrate current message.

*7. More Revealing and Appealing:* Visual aids are more revealing and appealing to the eyes. Figures are dry hard to eyes but visuals are more attractive to the eyes fascinating and impressive. Numerical data may not leave a much lasting impression on the minds. Even a layman can understand the nature of pictures.

*8. Stimulating.* They can often generate interest by providing a contrast to the written or spoken text of the subject matter.

*9. Audience Participation:* The participatory approach in communication can be achieved through visual media. It involves audience participation to have effective interaction. The term participatory communication refers to the efforts along several lines to develop communication involving recipients of message. In this audience also affect the communicator. The audience or a part of audience play an effective role in communication.

*10. Saving Time:* Visual aids save lot of time as very little effort is sufficient to grasp, understand to draw meaningful inferences. The psychology of the human mind is that an individual may not like to go through or hard written words.

**Main Demerits**

Simultaneously, the visual aids also have their limitations and disadvantages which are enumerated below.

*1. Message Limitation:* At a time one picture, slide, chart, graph etc., can be shown. Only limited subject matter can be accommodated in each medium and only transmit a limited number of communication pieces. A congested presentation or heavy message load may result in the risk of confusion.

*2. Preparation:* Preparation of visual pictures takes a lot of time. It requires technical and expert people to draw, print or paint.

*3. Cost:* The main limitation of the media is that it is costly matter to use. This is the reason for not using visual aids in majority of the cases. It involves not only heavy installation cost but also recurring revenue cost. The real criterion for not using by majority is the cost.

4. *Time:* The media, though simple and attractive to see is not so easy in practice because it takes lot of time, effort in their preparation. The preparation of subject matter of discussion or text or oral report is invariably be quicker to produce than visual aids. It requires lead time to prepare.

5. *Personal Preference:* Certain people dislike or are suspicious of graphs, either because they have been conditioned to believe that high technical skill is necessary to their understanding, or because they consider that printed numbers automatically invest them with a degree of authority that is lost immediately they are displayed in graphical form.

6. *Approximation:* Approximations and adjustments, round of figures are the common features in preparation of charts or graphs. Pinpoint accuracy in the presentation of message is not possible in all circumstances. It gives some sort of confusion and communication gap.

**Audio-Visual Communication**

Literally the word 'Audio' means sound or hearing. Visual means sight or the process of seeing. A new sophisticated mass communication technology capable or producing sounds and pictures. It is possible to visualise from it or to form a clear picture of something in the mind. Television, pictures, films etc., that are used as aids to learning. Audio-visual aids are used mostly in teaching, conferences. Recent development in audio-visual devices are revolutionising communication systems. Many audio-visual devices have come up for use and new modes of access to information are emerging. These devices have relevance for the distance communication, their potential has yet to be fully recognised and exploited particularly by all large-scale business organisations. The recent devices are the video and the audio-synchronised slide projector units, which screen programmes, often referred to as audio-visuals. Audio-visual aid is an effective means of communication. A newly developed highly sophisticated communication technology widely practiced in recent years by the large and complex business organisation, educational institutions and government departments. Audio means sound or hearing, as mentioned above is just only an aid to visual communication.

It helps to bridge the communication gap. Audio-visual technique is a tool to give effect and impression to effective communication. Audio in relation to visual implies interpretation, explanation, and narration of the pictures, photo, slides, film etc., shown and used as a means of communication having both the qualities of seeing and hearing.

Visual communication is not complete unless it is supplemented by comments, narration, explanation, interpretation to be given by the transmitter or the communicator at appropriate stage where slide is shown. Audio-visual aids combine both the advantages and meet complete and effective communication. Just seeing the visual aids does not satisfy the much needed explanation required by the observer on the visual aids. While observing, a piece of explanation is expected by the observer to form full opinion and understanding.

Therefore, audio-visual aids have been widely used in recent years. In precise manner, it may be mentioned that business houses have in recent years do much rely upon audio-visual aids to bridge the communication gap and as a means to effective communication. They are really and greatly helpful to the enterprises in achieving its desired goals. This media brings people together and closer and to get people well informed with the objectives, and plans of the organisation.

**Uses and Merits**

In fact, the management is adopting this aid within the organisation:

(1) To inform and help people working in production sections knowing the different sophisticated techniques, produces and methods or production.

(2) The industrial and business houses do much depend upon this technique to apprise people working at the front line about the discharge of organisation's goals and social responsibilities.

(3) To inform people within the organisation about the people working in other organisations for comparison.

(4) The government can inform the public about national objectives, plan progress, achievements, development schemes etc.

(5) Educational Institutions can use them as an effective medium to impart instructions.

(6) Managerial functions like planning, control, direction and motivation can be effectively discharged.

(7) Help to arrive at a correct decision and formulate a policy.

(8) Extensively can be used for broadcasting adult educational programmes, to impart education especially at elementary level, and to have a clear communication with the villagers.

(9) Both commercial and non-commercial mass publicity, mass propaganda, education, opinion and research can be taken up.

(10) To educate people in general about any specific development in any particular area.

(11) To get the people informed about the message of the communication.

(12) To depict a clear idea with possible narration, explanation, interpretation, comment etc., which makes it easily understandable.

The success of organisational efforts in group activities very much depends upon the choice of tools and techniques and their application thereof for the solution of its problems. Urban areas have a fairly well developed system of mass-media. It is, therefore, necessary to device a clear communication method to reach villages. The villages are unlettered, various other audio-visual media like simple and striking posters with appropriate illustrations and slogans, mobile vans fitted with public address system, will constitute one form of media. In communication planning today, a move towards a scientific system is simultaneous with proposal to induct the new media into information programme.

The media provide a technological tool for substituting for, or extending the reach of the traditional communication system. The aids provide an opportunity and the occasion for the induction of instruction, direction, coordination and motivation reform. The language of the programmes telecast over media is important consideration. We have 14 recognised languages and there are many unrecognised languages and dialects. Local or regional languages should be given priority.

From Indian context a number of factors affect language selection such as time-sharing of the satellite arranging for suitable translations and transcreations of programmes, and ensuring a minimum qualitative standard and so on. It is more appropriate to emphasise in this regard that in order to achieve the desired objectives of effective communication and to deliver the goods properly, the language selected should be lucid, clear, precise, easily understandable and in tune with the popular use.

The visual media like pictures, slides, films should be attractive, of educational value, capable of creating impression, long-memorising element, straight approach, to convey the message of ideas, facts, opinions etc., and to arrange them orderly without technical jargons. The timing factor of programme telecast is also equally to be emphasised. Otherwise the message may not reach to the target. Therefore, timing should be convenient for the people to whom the broadcast is meant for, programmes should be properly arranged, and they should not be too long or too short.

In order to make the audio-visual media more effective and useful, it should be necessary to:

1. have sufficient autonomy in developing and broadcasting programme.
2. provide special channels and frequencies for villages, and for educational programmes.
3. have professionals and talented people to produce good programmes.
4. constitute expert group which can monitor and evaluate the programmes to bring improvement.

## Video

A modern technology can greatly enrich oral message relating to Television and Radio. A word applied to all visual aspects of television signals, equipment etc. In common usage, for video recording or for any machine that can be used to record and playback such recordings, such as video cassettes, recorders, video tape recorders etc. Prior to 1966 a good quality black and white video recorder and player cost anywhere between 50,000 and 1,00,000 U.S. dollars.

A massive break through in this technology has taken place in the mid 1960s and by 1970s good VCRs were available for about 1,00 U.S. dollars. In India today it is possible to acquire a colour monitor and VCR for about twenty thousand rupees and the prices may go down further in the years to come. VCRs have already made mass use in the entertainment field and also made a modest beginning in the educational field. Video based instruction is already in sue in advanced countries. The experience and facilities in the United States are of some interest. As of 1980, video-taped lectures for 450 courses prepared by a faculty drawn from 22 universities were available to the interested users.

A National Technological University has been established and it offers on-campus as well as off-campus instructional television courses through video programming, which enable students to work towards a master's degree programme. Video-cassettes are available for programmes produced in the studio as well as those produced through recording of candid classroom instruction sessions. A remarkable development in India has been the production facilities for preparation of video instructional packages as set up in some universities. There are many advantages in video use for communication. Among its advantages which one may mention is the richness of the media in conveying instructional material using visual images, colour, sound and special effects.

A major drawback noted is a terms of the lack of interaction between the teacher and the student. Except for special situations, if one treats video-based instruction, not as a substitute for a existing arrnagement of live-instruction, but as an aid, there is little dispute regarding its utility. For many special situations, video-based instruction can also successfully serve as a substitute for live-instruction. It is high time, therefore, that engineering education in India begins to explore the potential of this new technology for making instruction more effective and widely accessible. Video programmes are more expensive than slide programmes. Video programmes are simpler to play back as one does not have to undertake the laborious process of mounting slides.

Other advantages are duplication is cheaper and of two types, namely, studio production and the candid classroom production which is an impromptu presentation. In case of studio production complete script is to be prepared prior to recording. A number of video programmes have been produced in India in educational information field. It has been under the aegis of the Curriculum Development Cell of Civil Engineering Department at IIT Delhi, using production facilities at IIT and the Mass Communication Research Centre of Jamia Millia. The video programmes are: Alterberg's Limits, consolidated undrained Traixial Test with pore water pressure Measurement; Dewatering of Sub-soil using wellpoint system, construction of under-Reamed Pile Foundations.

**Audio Cassette**

One of the advanced technology in information technology which is presently available in the market and is in popular use and gaining importance throughout the world. Among others, the materials used for audio and television can be supplied in the form of audio-cassettes. Audio-cassettes can be stored. It has been found to be very useful as a tool of self-learning, as a means for executive training, and as an aid for continuing education. Audio means sound or hearing. Audio cassette is also used in recent years as the most useful teaching medium.

These enable the learner to have control over the learning materials. The learner can listen to the cassettes according to his own convenience. It can be stopped at any time. Another advantage of audio-cassette over radio is re-use over a section of the tape whenever he wants and it can be used again and again for revision or recall. Photograph records and flexidiscs are further developments in this matter. An obvious advantage of the audio cassettes over the radio programmes is that they are under the control of the user. Students can stop the player to take rest, make notes or can replay a difficult section.

A study of the Distance Teaching at Thailand's Sukhothai Thammathirat Open University (STOU) gives us an idea of the different purposes the audio cassette can be used for. STOU used the tapes to,

(a) provide orientation of the course,
(b) clarify certain complex ideas,
(c) give feedback to the student's activities and assignments,
(d) summarise major ideas of each unit, and
(e) present the views of external experts.

Massey University (New Zealand) tried using cassette tapes for tutorials in History. Groups of learners listened to a lecture on the tape. Then they would discuss the given questions and record the conclusion on the tape. They sent this tape to the university which sent its comments either again on tape or through mail. Gwynn has analysed the results and they would be applicable to all the subjects where 'tutorial' forms an essential part and where no single answer is possible for a given question.

**Videotape**

A recording tape carrying pictures and sound. It is used to record programmes in pictures and sound using videotape. Videotape is a powerful alternative to conventional printing. Videotapes have literally taken over the entertainment world from Indian Cinema. Videotape store magnetic signals for simultaneous subsequent retrieval of the visual and the audial information components. Lectures by experts, demonstration of process/techniques and field trips of inaccessible/remote regions could be recorded on videotapes for subsequent use. TV series like 'Secrets of the Sea' and 'The Living Planet' illustrate the numerous possibilities of its use in OLS as well as FLS. Videodiscs have not been as popular as videotape in spite of their obvious advantage. Compared to videotape, videodisc "...represents the densest storage medium in existence.

It is very durable and because of the nature of the system, free from wear...its radial format provides almost instant access to anyone of 55,000 clear, sharp and rock-steady images, instead of having to wind foot after foot of video tape. Compared to videotape, videodisc recording is less cumbersome and though its front-end cost is much higher, it is almost thrice as cheap as videotape in the long run.

Video tape is a very useful innovation which removes the constraint of viewing TV programmes at a fixed time.

**Videotex**

The international name for the system originally designated *viewdata,* but also often taken to mean the broadcast service, generally known as Teletext. Sometimes, the term "broadcast videotex" is used for Teletext. The remarkable development in the electronic media, among others is videotex. This technology increases the capacity of the television set. It allows the home television set to function like a computer terminal and retrieve information and graphics from a remote data base. A videotex system would be very useful in disseminating general information about courses and programmes available through distance education. Word processors and text processors have made text-editing much less cumbersome and they now provide easy availability of simpler versions of text to suit the competence of individual learners.

Electronic publishing could be videotex-based. Videotex system comprises a telephone, a television set for monitoring, a computerfed data base, a key board controller and a modern unit 'Modern' is an acronym for a modulating—demodulating device because it converts a digital square-wave signal that cannot be processed by a telephone into an analogue signal that can be easily processed by it. It also provides for reverse function, i.e., conversion from the analogue into the digital form. The following figure represents a schematic diagram of a videotex system.

The listener/viewer operates the key controller and the oral information is available through modem over telephone and its visual counterpart is flashed on the T.V. screen. The telephone and modem allow for a two-way interactive system wherein the listener/viewer can ask questions, seek clarifications or get supplementary information. Prestel (Great Britain), Antiope (France), Captain (Japan) and Telidon (Canada) are good examples of successful videotex systems. Among these, prestal was the first to become a world videotex service in 1979. Teletext, on the other hand, provides for one-way facility. The listener/viewer cannot seek additional information. Videotex is relatively faster and provides easier access to and more fruitful use of computer database. Videotex thus holds greater promise for Indian Open Learning System. Information can be stored in large quantities in databases. The Council for Educational Technology of Great Britain provides a good example of a fast developing educational database. Large databases stored on mainframe computers with multiple access points can put learners in contract with an almost inexhaustible store-house of information.

The American Centre at New Delhi through its instant access to various databanks in the U.S. now makes available the latest information on almost any topic to any scholar who is sure of the nature of information on almost any topic to any scholar who is sure of the nature of information that he seeks. Data vendors like DIALOG, MEDILINE, MUXUS can be hooked on to the telecommunication network in the U.S.A. and made available to information seekers almost all over the globe. Therefore videotex is a transmission device system. It uses a T.V. set to display text. It helps to use the computer based information services.

Teletext and viewdata are the two kinds of video systems.

***(a) Teletext:*** Teletext refers to the transmission of text on the usual television channels. The system displays text on T.V. sets. The British Broadcasting Corporation

(BBC) and Independent Television (ITV) render pages of information when requested by the viewer. Teletext system is more popular in British region. On switching key pad and within a few seconds the required page appears on the screen. The system covers many specific topics like stock market, consumer prices, financial matters, weather information, economics, technology etc.

***(b) Viewdata:*** Viewdata is another type of videotex system. It is also computer based information system. The network operates by linking viewdata terminals to a central computer through telephone lines like in case of teletext on request by the viewer page appears on the screen or printer. Originally information is transmitted on pages.

**Videocassettes**

The technology is available and is gaining importance all over the world. The material used for radio and television can be supplied in the form of video cassettes. The video cassettes can be stored. In view of limitations of television increasing use is being made of video cassettes.

**Videodisc**

Video disc is a new development in the electronic media. It increases the capacity of the television set. Video disc is a system similar to the long playing record except that it carries both audio and video through the conventional television set. It has enormous storage capacity. The glossary of technical terms related to new technologies gives meaning of videodisc as a system for recording video information on a disk, similar to a long-playing record, which enables in to be replayed.

However such a system can also be used to record digital data and such discs can hold very larger amount of information, although the data can only be written once and, in order to amend data, it has to be re-written on a blank part of the disc. The optical disc has more enormous storage capacity. The optical disc can store, 1,08,000 tracks and 54,000 on each side. The entire Encyclopedia Britannica could be stored on a single disc with a room to spare. Usually called as disc communication videodiscs are other powerful alternatives to conventional printing.

**Disk**

A revolving device platter on which data and programmes are stored. A file, i.e., an organised collection of connected records, that resides on a magnetic disk. Disk drives is an electromechanical device that rotates magnetic disks, that writes data and reads data from a floppy disk. Disk pack ais a storage medium having multiple magnetic disks. Magnetic disks are popularly used device for direct access secondary storage. It is a metal or plastic platter like phonograph record. There are several types of magnetic disks. But all magnetic disks are round platters coated with a iron-oxide or other magnetizable recording materials. Disks are of different sizes. Such as larger 14 inches metal disk, same size metal disks packaged in removable cartridge or disk pack, small 8 inches and 5¼ inches rigid disk housed in winchester disk devices and same size portable floppy (flexible) disks, 4 inches compact floppy and rigid disks. On a magnetic disks there are no grooves, and data and information are stored on disks in a number of invisible concentric circles called Tracks. A drive which rotates a disk at a constant speed of between 3000 and 600 revolutions per minutes. Hard disks rotate at a speed from 2400 to 4700 revolutions per minute.

**Floppy Disk**

Though now obsolete, a computer device used to store

data and programmes is called as diskette. A low cost thin flexible disk coated with magnetic particles. A magnetic medium used for storage purpose. Standard disks are eight inches in diameter and the more common mini disks are about 5¼ inches. A mini disk has a storage capacity around 15 to 20 pages of a book, its special quality is that it is flexible, flat, that magnetically records and provides access to stored data. Contrast with floppy disk is hard disk which is a rigid metal platter coated with magnetic particles. Optimal disk is a device used with laser reading or writing to store huge quantities of data. The source document data to be keyed directly into a floppy magnetic disk. It is called floppy disk because it is made out of flexible plastic material. The plastic material is coated with iron-oxide recording substance and data are recorded as tiny invisible magnetic spots on this coating.

***Telidon:*** The Canadian Videotex service. It differences in a number of respects from the UK prestal Service, particularly in that the data is transmitted in the from of "picture description instructions" rather than as a serial character stream. AS those PDIs occupy more than one byte each it may be a less efficient method of transmitting data. But this is in fact, dependent on the data being transmitted. The graphics displayed are of a higher resolution than those possible in alpha-massaic system such as prestel. A Canadian video system. Technologically advanced countries have developed useful combination of cable T.V., electronic black board, fibre optics and telephone that converts a simple television set into a powerful and educational tool called the Telidon.

***Magnetic Tape:*** A magnetic storage device, utilises magnetic properties of materials to store data on such device. Such devices are disks tapes and chips. A magnetic tape is a tape or ribbon coated with a magnetic material on which data and information may be stored in the form of magnetically polarised spots. It has been used for decades as an input or storage medium, for batch processing. Today also it is used for high speed large volume batch application. Its advantages are high data density and fast transfer rate. The magnetic tape input medium is packaged in different ways. On a plastic ribbon iron-oxide or other magnetizable materials are coated. Tape in large reels is used in mini and mainframe computer systems. Magnetic tape cartridges are used in minicomputers. Magnetic tape cassettes are also used in minicomputers. Tape is similar to one used in a sound tape recorder. It is a plastic ribbon coated on one side with iron oxide or some other material. Both information, data and sound can be played back many times similar to the songs on a sound tape, the data and information records organised on a magnetic tape can be retrieved. Read or write heads are small electromagnets capable of reading, writing, or erase the polarised spots that represent data on magnetic tape.

***Cyclops:*** A British electronic system. Cyclops is a system devised to overcome the lack of visual support. This allows tutors and students to sue a light open to write or draw on an ordinary TV screen. The picture is converted digitally to a second signal and sent down a standard telephone line, where it is decoded and appears on the TV screen at the other end of the line. Prepared visual material (stored on audio cassettes) can also been sent down this line. It is an audio-visual teaching medium. The British Open University has developed an extremely versatile audio-visual teaching medium called cyclops which is based on the conventional TV set, standard audio cassettes and micro-computer technology. The cyclops can also be linked to a telephone and that increases its versatility as a teaching tool.

**Computer**

A household word at the toungue all over the world, a large mechanical and electronic contrivance with associated electro chemical equipments capable of carrying out mathematical functions at high speed and accuracy. Computer is capable of storing and processing huge quantity of information and performing calculations through data processing machine. Computer has been defined by the United States of American Institute, as a device capable of solving problems, by accepting data performing described operations on the data and supplying the results of the operations. Calculators, digital computers and analog computers are the types of computers. It has components like input unit, memory storage, arithmetic unit, output unit etc. Computing processing is done and controlled by a computer programming. It has separate language like Cobol, Fortran etc.

An electronic contrivance which solves problems and does complicated calculations by processing data according to prescribed, programmed instructions and then produces and or retains the outcome of these processes; one who computers; a reckoner; a calculator. (New Webster's Dictionary). According to M.K. Adler Computer is a machine for carrying out calculations of several stages automatically. May be Analogue Computer, which simulates, processes and produces results measured in physical quantities, or Digital Computer which carries out mathematical processes out by operations based on counting.

Computer is used for not only mathematical purposes, but has emerging role of communication, and in education particularly more in engineering education. It is an excellent device that can be fully employed. Computers are going to be the "Whizz-kids" of our future educational system. Computation, information storage, communication and control are the four major functions of most computers. Super computers are endowed with artificial intelligence and they are capable of intermediate level reasoning as well. Intricate calculations or multivariate data analysis become almost 'kid-stuff' with their help. Huge amounts of information can be very systematically stored in its memory (depending upon its memory size) for subsequent retrieval and use. Computers can provide flexible interaction with learners within the limits of the programme that defines their functional range. Computers can help us exercise extrafine control over various processes like satellite manoeuvring, satellite tracking and rocket launching. A computer memory may be of ROM (read only memory) or RAM (randum access memory) variety. The ROM variety is more widely used and its four sub types, viz., mask programmed ROMs used for storing programmes during its manufacture, PROMs (Programmable only once at manufacture stage), EPROMs (erasable programmable read only memories that can be programmed many times) and EAROMs (electrically alterable read only memories) have been described in detail by Hankridge and Bradbeer *et al.* Use of computers in education has resulted in CAL/CAI (Computer Assisted Learning/Instruction). Arrival of computers in American classrooms has been compared to an avalanche. A variety of computer languages both low level and high level (algebraic) enables users to work with various computers, e.g., ADA, APL, BASIC, COBOL, FORTRAN, LISP, PASCAL, PL/I, RPG-II, SNOBOL, SPITBOL, WATFOR, WATFIV, LOGO, etc. Computers can be immensely useful in providing individualised repetitive or analogous practice to learners, problem-solving exercises as well as activities for developing a variety of skills in a training programme. Project Class should prove a catalyst for increasing the use of computers in Indian education.

The computer is an excellent device that can be usefully employed for evaluating student's assignments. A fully developed computer Assisted Education System can be used for correction and comments on student's replies to multiple choice questions with carefully selected distractions. In this system, an optical reader 'corrects' the students' replies, after which the computer selects relevant comments and explanations from among a great number of those programmed and stored for the purpose. The computer also checks and refers to the individual student's answer or an unsatisfactory answer elicits different comments from the computer, depending on the way in which the student has misunderstood or wrongly combined items.

Sometimes even correct replies are commented upon to underline something important or to strengthen the motivation of the students. Encouraging and counselling comments based on the overall performance of the student are also provided by the computer. All this is typed by the computer into a personal letter addressed to the individual student. However, this use of the computer is restricted to the objective assignments of the multiple choice type. Therefore, a number of subjects, themes within subjects and general types of learning like free problem oriented learning would require live tutors. Even the multiple choice, questions which can be marked by the computer are not always suited for all kinds of learning outcomes. The greatest advantage of tutor-marked assignments is that it greatly reduces the average turn-round time of the assignments. The computer also eliminates the chances of erratic marking which has become the ban of our examination system. The computer ensures uniformity in evaluation.

**Computer Aided Design, Instruction and Learning**

The role of computers in engineering education cannot be overemphasised and needs no special elucidation. The computer assisted instruction involves the use of computers to perform instructional functions. In order to update the syllabus and improve the standards and to prepare the students to tackle the problems of the future, the curriculum must encompass latest technological advancement relating to Robotics, Computer Aided Design (CAD) and Computer Aided Manufacturing (CAM). Computer based instructions include a broad range of application. But they can be divided into two types namely: (1) Direct Instructions (2) Instructional Management. The first type is called as Computer Assisted or aided Instruction, and the second type is called as Computer Managed Instruction. Some of the features of these two systems are:

*I. Computer Assisted/Aided Instruction:* It covers a number of activities such as drill and practice, tutoring, simulations, gaming, enquiry, dialogue, information retrieval and problem solving. It is relating to educational concept which emphasises the student in conversational form with a computer which has programme formulated in advance. It perform any instructional function presenting materials, problem situations, guiding a student's thinking by answering his questions, assessing his performance, managing his path through a course of selecting the material to be presented or by assigning tasks to be performed away from the computer, or any combination of these. Alternatives through instructional units are programmed into the computer. Besides machine directed activities as mentioned above it includes machine student dialogue, counselling, guidance. In sum it is the use of computers on time shared basis to carry out many instructional management function.

*II. Computer Managed Instruction:* It includes instructional support functions such as testing prescribing, record keeping, scheduling, monitoring and time and resource management. The machine discharges, the functions to monitor the instructional process. The object in its use is to provide diagnostic and prescriptive information to the instructor to guide him in making instructional decisions. It takes advantage of conventional data processing equipment.

Computer Aided (Assisted) Assessment, Examination, Test (CAE/CAT), Computer Aided Design (CAD), Computer Aided Learning (CAL) and Computer Managed Learning (CML) or some of the new developments in education communication. In the days to come emerging role of computers in Engineering education would be very great.

## Types of Computers

Based on the type of data processed, a computer may be classified into the following categories:

*1. Analog Computer:* An analog computer is a device that operates on data by measuring changes in continuous physical variables like voltage, resistance, rotation etc. It operates or data in the mode of continuously variable physical quantities. An analog computer is used when data is processed continuously such as monitoring temperature, pressure. It is opposed to digital computer.

*2. Digital Computer:* A device in contrast with analog computer. A digital computer is used when data are discrete. It manipulates discrete data and performs arithmetic and logic operations on the data. In other words it operates on digital data.

*3. Hybrid Computer:* A type of computer which combines the features of both digital and analog computers. A data processing technique which utilises both analog and digital representation of data. It handles both discrete and continuous data.

**Other Types of Computers**

*1. Mini Computer.* A small general purpose computer such as desk top size, and four drawer file cabinet. The term mini means small which has smaller memory capacity as well as input, output capacities. Comparing other computers mini computer is lower in cost, less speed and smaller in size. It is to be distinguished from micro processor, which is smaller than minicomputer. But it is continued to use and apply to small general purpose computes. However, the difference between minicomputers and micro-computers is very thin.

The physical size of the PDP-11 is six feet high and occupies 14 by 18 inches of floor space. This does not include a printer but does include storage devices like the magnetic cassette and the Floppy disk. Comparing medium sized or large scale computers minis originally meant low speed, small memory, less software and few peripheral units. The minis are 16-bit machine. There are 32-bit super mini models. Earlier mini computers were applied to a single purpose specialised such as to monitor instruments or to control a machine tool or general applications in small concerns. But today mini computers are applied to complex situations. They are the most popular data processing system in business concerns.

*2. Micro Computer.* A smallest device of computer. It

consists of a micro processor, storage and input output elements. A micro processor is a technique that provides the basic arithmetic, logic and control circuits necessary for processing. A micro computer with micro-processors which is given additional memory and input output capabilities, then it is called as micro computer. It is a general purpose processing device. Small in size, a computer on a chip to a small typewriter size. They are easily carried from one place to another and can be placed on a small desk. The usual storage devices like magnetic tape cassettes, floppy disks etc., can be used as external storage medium. It forms an important part of the integrated information system. Today they are used in all types of organisations, small or big, schools, offices, banks, homes and other office works.

Micros can be linked to a big computer. The distinction between a micro computer and mini computer is that a mini is originally designed to serve multiple users simultaneously.

*3. Main Frame Computer:* These computers have greater storage capacity and offer faster processing speed comparing other types of computer. In size main frame computers are ranging from small to a very large. The smaller main frames and super minis perform on a similar scale. But a main frame is more powerful than a typical mini and hence often called as main frame. In centralised data processing system main frame computers are used in many organisations. A number of users can work simultaneously as they support a large number of terminals. Word processors are used as terminals. They prepare thousands of paychecks, invoices, making labels etc. The main part of the computer usually referred to the Central Processing Unit. The entire series of a mainframe models of small and large are typically lumped together under a family designation by mainframe manufactures. It permits to carry programmes framed for one machine on other models in the same family. Mainframes have been playing an important and vital role in information processing.

*4. Personal Computer (PC):* As the name indicates, a computer originally designed and oriented towards single use. It denotes the use of computers by individuals. A general purpose compute system. It carries programme instructions to perform a wide variety of tasks, which possess all the functional components available in larger systems. They are usually found in the home management, personal productivity. A TV set can be used to display output. It has a limited primary storage capacity. PCs can be used not only for game programme but enables the user to acquire computer literacy. They give an opportunity to become familiar about computers as to how, and when to use and utilities.

Today they came in a variety of configurations side by side using television and cassette player. They are available today in different shapes and sizes like portable models, notebook sized, briefcase sized, desk-top models, transportables, etc. They are called single-user-oriented because, most of personal computers are designed to be used by one person at a time. In recent years another system has emerged, they are multi-user oriented.

*5. Super Computer:* A super computer is characterised by its very high processing speed, very large size, more storage capacity, powerful and costly computer. Only a few organisations can afford and use super computer because of prohibitive cost and processing capacity. They are of national importance and used in big scientific research and development fields like energy, space exploration, medicine, industrial technological areas like aircraft. A super computer holds 64 bits of information, so, applied to a complex computation.

It is very costly, between 4 million to 15 million dollars. Gray Research and Control Data Corporation (CDC) are the important concerns producing super computers in USA. So a powerful device applied to making top secret weapons research calculations, complex calculations for petroleum and recasting problems, earth's atmosphere etc. Data of complex nature are fed into super computers.

Human thinking of ideas and artificial intelligence is the relation of human-machine communication process. A computer uses many devices to communicate with human beings. The following are the various system components in a computer towards electronic message transmission.

**1. Input**

Input in relation to computer denotes devices, media and techniques used in process of human machine communication. Pertaining to computer channel involved in the insertion of information into a processing system. There are input devices which permit direct human-machine communication. There are some input devices which require information to be recorded on a magnetisable materials such as floppy disks, magnetic tapes etc. The keyboard, the mouse, input pen, touch screen, microphone, central processing unit or components used for communication between a person and computer system.

**2. Processor**

Process means a systematic series of operations to achieve a desired result. Processor is the main component and is the heart of the computer system. A processor unit is capable of performing operations upon information inserted. There are three sections such as primary storage section, arithmetic log section and control section. In order to solve limited storage capacity of the primary storage section, a computer may have secondary capabilities known as secondary storage devices which have connected directly to the processor.

### 3. Output

Relating to a device or process involved in the transfer of information out of information inserted into a processing system. It is information transferred from internal storage of a computer to any device outside the computer. The process works for taking information out of the computer. Output devices are instruments of interpretation and communication between a person and computer. Display screens, desk top printers, magnetic tap output device, printer, graphics plotter, visual display of online work station, laser printers, micro film are some of the output devices.

### Computer Communication Language

A computer has a machine language which is used directly by a computer. Language is a set of rules adopted to convey information. A language used to express programme is termed as programming language. So rules used to convey message or data. It is a system of communication which includes all the symbols, characters, and rules to be followed while communicating with computer. The machine language of a computer consists of strings of binary numbers by which the processor can directly understand. Assembly language translates the specified operation code symbol into its machine-language. High level language is a computer programming language which is nearer to natural language. It is oriented towards a particular class of processing problems.

The natural letters, symbols or text can be used than by using the machine language consisting of strings of binary numbers (0s 1s). Most of the programmes are prepared today which are written in high level language. The following are some of the major high level in use:

**1. Basic**

The word basic stands for Beginners All-Purpose Symbolic Instruction Code (BASIC). It is a major high level programming language developed at Dartmouth College. It is widely and popularly used programming language with personal computers and intime sharing systems. It is an interactive language, popular because it is easy to use. It allows direct communication between the computer system and the user during the preparation and use of programme. A person with little or no knowledge of computers of programming can learn to write basic programme. Within a short period of time one can learn. Data entering is easy. It is known of simplicity. Recreational and educational programmes are usually documented in basic. School students, engineers, business managers etc., popularly use basic.

**2. Fortran**

It stands for Formula Translator. A high level procedure oriented programing language used to perform mathematical computations. It is also widely used to draw programmes that perform mathematical computations for scientific, engineering, statistical and selected business applications. Most of the computers now in service can use Fortran. A standard language. It consists a series of statements which supply input-output, calculations, logic, comparison and other basic instructions to the machine. A compact language serves the requirements of scientists, engineers and business statisticians for business application.

**3. Cobol**

The term stands for Common Business Oriented Language. A specially designed business data processing language. A similar high level language for business application. This language is now the most widely used language for large business application. Conference of Data Systems Languages (CODASYL) is a group of representatives of computer manufactures, government agencies, user organisation, and Universities who developed and maintain the COBOL Language. The CODASYL Short Range Committee which prepared the COBOL frame work. It can be used in business data processing and can be used with personal computers. It has four divisions such as,

1. identification division,
2. environment division,
3. data division and
4. procedure division.

The advantage of COBOL language are:

1. It can be written in a quasi English form.
2. It can be followed more easily by the non-programmers in business.
3. It does not require much documentation.
4. It manipulates alphabetic characters in a better way than Fortran. There are many COBOL business applications modules and packages.

**4. PL/1**

Stands for programming Language/1. A similar high level general purpose programming language. It is procedure oriented language designed to combine features of COBOL, Fortran, Algol etc. It processes both scientific as well as file processing applications. It is best suited to solve a variety of business as well as scientific problems. The American National Standards Institute Committee produced PL/1 standard in 1976, in which are found features which exist in both Fortran and Cobol but it is flexible and sophisticated language. The language is more difficult to learn in its totality than Fortran or Cobol.

**5. RPG**

The letters stand for Report Programme Generator. A problem Oriented language designed to generate output reports. It uses a generator to construct programmes that produce reports and function other data processing activities. A file can be updated periodically. It is specialised with file description, input specifications, calculations output. The languages is very easy to learn and use. The formal rules are limited comparable with other languages. It is more useful to generate output reports. It is an important language of small business computer.

**6. Algol**

Standards for ALGORITHMIC language. It is widely used in Europe. It was first introduced in 1958. It is an international procedure oriented language designed by a group of international mathematicians and developed by groups in Europe and the United States. It is designed and intended for use primarily for scientific and mathematical applications.

**7. Pascal**

A widely used high level computer programming language. It is named in honour of Blaise Pascal, a French mathematician, philosopher and an inventor. It is designed for use of structured programming devices. It off spring of algol, is a similar building programme found in other languages.

**8. Ada**

A similar high level computer programming language. The language is sponsored by the U.S. Department of Defence (DOD) for use in military services. The language is named in honour of Lady Augusts Ada Lovelase, daughter of Lord Byron.

**9. Logo**

An educational language developed by Seymour Papert in 1960s. It is widely used for scientific research tasks particularly in Universities. It can be used by children to achieve talent, intellectual growth and acquire problem solving skills. They can communicate with a computer and learn graph, raw, colour and animate images.

# 7
# Mass Communication and MIS

"No good work whatever can be perfect, and the demand for perfection is always a sign of misunderstanding of the ends of art."

—*John Ruskin*

MIS (management information system) is basically a term widely used in the field of management. Since information dissemination in emphatic way is the prime concern of communication, here it is must for a media person to understand the management information system is pros and cons. We have tried here to furnish all salient features of MSS in systematic way.

According to Hussain and Hussain, "An information system is an organised set of components designed to produce intelligence required for decision-making. In a business context, the information is for management. The system itself has four main components: input, output, computer programmes and the processor.

As per Donald H. Sanderz, "A management information system (MIS) is a network of computer-based data processing procedures, developed in an organisation and integrated with manual and other procedures for the purpose of providing timely and effective information to support decision-making and other necessary management functions.

We will use a business example to illustrate some of the elements in this definition, but MIS concepts certainly aren't restricted to business."

According to Jerome Kanter, "A management information system (MIS) is a system that aids management in making, carrying out, and controlling decisions. Decision-making, including the process leading up to the decision can be termed planning, and management can be defined as the planning and control of the physical and personnel resources of the company in order to reach company objectives."

Basically there are three basic words in the caption, namely, management, information and system. It is an essential part of the study to understand the meaning of these words. The word management means the art of managing things and getting the things done through other people. It is an art and a profession. The functions of management are planning, organising, staffing, directing, controlling, coordination. The organisations have managers who plan, set goals and direct to accomplish the goals of the organisation. The functions of the managers differ according to the position occupied, namely, high, middle or low level.

Management have three levels, namely:

1. Top level management known as strategies management;
2. Middle level management called as tactical level; and
3. Low level management or supervisory level, also called as operating level. The last level is called as first line managers in charge of the employees. Top managers are responsible for overall operation

of the organisation. They are top executives variously called as chief executive officer, president, chairman. They formulate broad policies and objectives of the organisation. Middle level managers are under direct control of the top managers. They are functional managers, each function is headed by manager. The functions are Finance, Accounting, Personnel, Marketing, Production, headed by a person having specialised knowledge of the function. In the organisation structure they are positioned horizontally. Operating level implement the policies of top management routed to them through middle level managers.

The main principles of management are:

1. Division of work.
2. Authority and responsibility.
3. Discipline.
4. Unity of command.
5. Unity of direction.
6. Subordination of individual interests to general interest.
7. Remuneration.
8. Centralisation.
9. Scalar chain.
10. Order.
11. Equity.
12. Stability.
13. Initiative.
14. Esprit de corps.

The word information implies facts told or knowledge gained or given. Information with reference to management means knowledge which the managers at different levels receive or give at a given time. It is necessary to make distinction between data, information and communication. The word data is the plural of datum, which means fact! Facts or information given from which other facts may be worked out. The facts are data, the raw materials of information. The facts are by symbols like words spoken or written, visual, action and figures. Information is not data, the data comprise of information. Data are presented by symbols, but they are not information except in a limited sense. As used in data processing in computer, information is data arranged in an order and form useful to the people who receive it. So information is relevant knowledge, produced, as the output of data processing operations and acquired by people to enhance understanding and to achieve specific purposes. Computer data processing converts raw data into information. All information consists of data, but not all data produce specific and meaningful information. The managerial functions like planning, organisation, control and coordination etc., can be discharged effectively and smoothly only when necessary information is given to the managers, who can make timely and correct decision. A timely supply of information is indispensable to make a best judgement. While communication is a process of transmission of matter by symbols. All communication consists information, but not all information is capable of communication. Communication is only a piece of information which is very comprehensive in scope. Information is like an enormous umbrella, a broad concept which covers communication as one particular type of information. Information is a global concept referring to any pattern of energy input you are exposed to. Information includes both internal and external information. Today information is a factor of production like, capital labour etc.

The word system means an arrangement of many parts that work together. The establishment of arrangement of things relating to management. A system is a group of parts that are integrated to achieve desired objective. A system has more than one element. The other two important characters of a system are integrated parts and having a common purpose of a achieving some objective. It is "a grouping of integrated methods and procedures united to form an organised entity; an organised grouping of people, methods, machines, and materials collected together to accomplish a set of specific objectives." Computer has a group of integrated parts that have the common purpose of performing the operations.

According to Hussain and Hussain:

1. a group of interrelated or interacting elements;
2. a group of interrelated components that seeks the attainment of a common goal by accepting inputs and producing outputs in an organised process;
3. an assembly of methods, procedures, or techniques united by regulated interaction to form an organised whole;
4. an organised collection of people, machine, and method required to accomplish a set of specific functions. Thus input, output and processing devices are the three important components of system.

After having understood the three concepts presented above, it is clear now the concept of "Management Information System." It implies a system designed to provide information to different level managers required to manage and to accomplish organisational goals through effective decision-making. An organisation is a process of continuous decision-making, a complex, dynamic and interacting. The key factors needed in a decision process are the information input. The timely availability of relevant internal information, new and additional and enteral information helps to make effective decisions. Therefore, the primary objective in developing a total management information system should be the production of detailed up-to-the minute summaries of the past data and the use of them to project the future activity.

Different managerial levels need different types of information to take decisions effectively. Alternatively, modern complex business organisations, or, on the growth of an organisation, more levels may be needed comparable to smaller organisation. It is, therefore, necessary to provide different types of information to managers at different levels. Top-level-managers who make major policies, objectives, to them is necessary to supply objective information concerning general understanding of the organisation. Middle-level managers who implement the top-level plans, need such information to control, coordinate, allocate scarce resource and to select a particular course of action among available alternatives and the relative consequences of indifferent alternatives available to them. Operational decisions are made by the lower level managers, need detailed information relating to day-to-day operations. Computer technology is required for computerised information system.

Computerised information enables decision-making more effective. Decision Support Systems (DSSs) are the components of Management Information System. They are simulation, expert system and information centres. The designing of information system is based on what type of information is needed, why and for whom. Computer-based Management Information Systems help managers in decision-making process in a number of business areas. The business areas are raw materials, policy making, pricing, advertisements, research, accounting policies, investment decisions, product planning, marketing strategies, finance etc. Thus "An MIS supports the planning and decision-making activities of many managers."

Simulation is a trial and error problem solving approach that is very useful in planning. Simulation models serving managers at different levels may also be integrated into an overall corporate modelling approach to planning and decision-making. An expert system is a software package that includes:

1. a stored base of knowledge in a specialised are and
2. the capability to probe this knowledge base and make decision recommendations.

An organisation may have established information centre. The centre gives its users a direct online path into the organisation's data bases to retrieve the facts they need.

**Electronic Mail/Message Systems (EMMS)**

Presently messages are forwarded through postal service or sent verbally over telephone line. The computer systems now avoid the usual postal service. There are many problems associated with postal services such as:

(1) The cost of sending a message through postal service is increasing.

(2) It is known that postal service is relatively slow.

(3) Often messages get lost sometimes.

In order to overcome the problems of usual postal services the "Electronic Mail/Message Systems" have emerged. The EMMS is also called as "Computer Mail/ Message System." (CMMS). The EMMS or CMMS is a network that can store, transmit and deliver messages by electronic means. Because it has several advantages and overcoming the problems in case of usual postal services the EMMS has gained much popularity in most of the advanced countries. Even using telephone for message transmission there is no certainty that the message reaches the recipient. The presence of the recipient and willingness to take and interpret the call in the same sense are the problems associated with it.

The EMMS network has been developed with a view to solve some of the problems in message distribution system. The new concept or network facilitates transmission of large message load or information considerably at high speed. Many devices like telephone lines and hookup devices etc., are used to connect distance locations. An Electronic Computer Originated Mail (E-COM) is a postal service system available in US. Under the electronic means the terminal or computer of the customer transmits messages with high speed, quickly, economically and accurately. The computer of receiving post office records the message, where the message is printed on a printer. The printed message is then delivered to the addressee. The advantages of this network are it saves typing time, addressing, mailing etc.

The mail/message systems by electronic means provide a number of functions. The system provides services like:

(a) message distribution system,

(b) transmission of documents, and pictures,

(c) computerised conferences.

**Transmission of Pictures**

Like message pictures can be transmitted by using special machines known as "Fascimile machines" or "Fax machines." Under electronic mail message systems an original document containing photographs, maps, charts and other drawings are transmitted by placing in a sending facsimile machine. The computer based fascimile systems are more useful in modern offices. The sending machine scans document containing pictures and the receiving device reproduces the scanned picture or image.

**Message Distribution Service**

In a message distribution services, a message is transmitted to a recipient who has a device called as 'Electronic Mail Box." A written message is keyed into the system. The Voice Mail System (VMS) holds recorded voice message.

**Transmission of Text**

The telex system has been in use for transmitting messages through teleprinter exchange network. This is an old or conventional method for transmission of text. In this EMMS function, text is transmitted over telecommunication lines. There are two terminals in this system known as teleprinters which appear like typewriters. There are two devices, sending end terminal and receiving and teleprinter. These two distant terminals are connected at the sending end terminal, the message is keyed into the key board. The receiving end teleprinter prints the message so transmitted over the lines by the sending end terminal.

In this EMMS function the teleprinter terminals are connected to computers. Computer is also used in transmission of text. The text is keyed and appears on the screen. Under this system it is possible to check the message before transmission.

**Teleconferencing**

Also known as telephone conference-discussions in which practically all direct communication between the participants is carried out via the public telephone system. It is an arrangement which facilitates the speakers to communicate each other in different locations using public telephone links. Participants of the conference located in different geographical distance areas can discuss issues by using their terminals that are linked together via a telecommunication network. It helps them greatly to communicate voice, text and video signals. It is an electronic linking of geographically scattered people who are participating at the same time. It refers to the meeting of people who are geographically separated, but under this system all participating in discussions through a telecommunication system. It uses two-way voice, text or video communication equipment. Under this system the participants can interact, interface over wide distance in real time.

In recent years, big business organisations are using teleconferencing method to conduct business meetings with the concerned executives who are geographically scattered all over a region. For instance a firm having a chain of branch offices offers a network for teleconference service. The members or participants can go to their local branch and participate, and interact in discussions with the speaker, at other branches. It may be mentioned that an alternative to computer conferencing is teleconferencing. An electronic linkage of geographically scattered people, is no doubt a oral communication through a medium but without presence of persons.' The advantages of face-to-face conversation cannot be obtained from teleconferencing which cannot replace them. Body movements, facial expressions which also communicate feelings, attitudes etc., cannot be seen with teleconferencing. But, on the other hand, teleconferencing offers a number of advantages like:

(1) Time is saved.
(2) Cost and energy are saved.
(3) Travel to distant place to attend conference is eliminated.
(4) No monotony or fatigue.

Participants in the teleconferencing can use fascimile devices, electronic blackboards which give chalk impressions to be reproduced on distant T.V. monitors, picturephone meeting service, and other communicating technologies to transmit opinions, facts, feelings, figures etc., over a wide distance in real time. This system literally passes papers, back and forth to one another as they talk, argue, debate, exchange, interact the important points.

This development of telecommunication resulted in TV meetings, save travel, cost, time and wearying business trips. It helps in two-way-television system, fact-to-face conversation with people at widely separated locations. The American Telephone and Telegraph (AT and T) company operates picture phone meeting service. It is possible to link 11 conference facilities that are part of the picture phone meeting service operated by At and T company. They are located in Atlanta, Boston, Chicago, Dallas, Los Angeles, New York City, Philadelphia, Pittsburgh, Sacramento, San Francisco and Washington.

## Computer Based Conferences

In teleconferencing it is necessary that all the participants of a conference to be present or to be on line at the same time. The system uses audio and video equipment for communication. The requirement of all the participant to be on line at the same time often poses problems. Under computerised teleconferencing it is not necessary for all the participants to be on line at their terminals or personal computers at the same time. Similarly it facilitates that it is also not necessary that the participants be physically present at the same place. A computer based teleconferencing permits the participants to attend meetings at their convenience or permits conferences to be held at the convenience of the participants.

The electronic mail/message system (EMMS) is a device which can be used to store and deliver by electronic means, messages which otherwise would be sent over telephone lines. An EMMS system is capable of performing a number of functions among them computerised conferences is one. The computer conference known as a computer based teleconferencing permits that the conference dialogue can be stored in computes.

A participant can sit at a terminal or personal computer at a convenient time and call up any conversation not seen, make comments if any, reply to questions. The special feature of this system is many participants can speak at the same time. Thousands of people at different geographical areas can use the system. The system requires that each participant is expected to have an access to a computer terminal connected to the conference network. The participant can sit at the terminal or personal computer at a convenient time and call up any conversation and respond to any message.

There is a data base facility in the system possessing a large number of text messages. The conversation or message is entered by a member of the computer conference, which is then made available to the other members of the conference. The participant can directly write his conversation, messages and comments which will be stored in computers. It is surprising to note that in developed countries computer based conferencing has been increasingly used. There are many computer conferencing networks developed for service. For example, the Informedia Corporation of Palo Alto, USA provides two computer conference facilities known as Planet and Notepad. Similarly New Jersey Institute of Technology, USA offers conference services on their network known as Electronic Information Exchange System. In order to use these services any member of a group has to dial local access telephone number, couples the telephone to a terminal. All group members can share a file. Under these systems the subscribers are grouped topic wise or groups according to their specific topic of interest such as technology, economics, etc.

A subscriber who is interested in many topics may join to more than one group. Group members may belong to corporations, governments, local authorities, hospitals, educational institutions and other non-profit organisations. The Stockholm University in Sweden offers another system known as COM in two languages, Swedish and English.

Computer based electronic mail/message systems offer a number of advantages. A few of them are:

(1) A lot of time is saved.

(2) A person can sit down at a terminal according to his convenient time.

(3) It avoids extensive travel and stay to attend in a conventional conference.

(4) It saves money and energies of a group of participants.

(5) They can attend on other important works.

(6) It maintains a permanent history of all conference discussions. The discussions are recorded and stored in a computer.

(7) It permits which message or conversation each participant has already seen.

(8) When operated it displaces all the conference entries which have not been seen.

(9) A person can directly read and write at convenient time.

(10) Message are stored in a computer.

Thus government and business organisation can use profitably computer based conference to conduct periodic meetings, transmission of ideas, opinions, facts etc.

**Telelecture**

In Oral Communication telephone is the most popular method. Telelecture is an arrangement which enables a speaker or lecturer to communicate with several classes or meetings or conferences in different locations simultaneously, using public telephone links. A best technique for making audio/visual presentation at distance. With a arrangement of telephone department there is hook up from a speaker's office to a meeting place or class room or conference where visuals can be shown while the speaker is heard. Telephone is used in distance communication to have interface between the speaker and the listener. In several advanced countries telephone are used in distance education to provide interaction between the tutors and students. In a country like India where telephones are not within the reach of ordinary man these cannot be used in all communications. With the help of two-way hook up facility members of audience can put questions to the speaker. There are countries which are using audio conference and video conferencing. For instance, in Canada, teleconferencing is being used in several education programmes, including professional development courses, in medicine, law, teacher education, health science, business and management.

In addition to the telephone being useful for teaching purposes it can be effectively used to improve management and administration not only in educational institutions but also for efficient and effective communication in large business organisations.

The expression word processing is pertaining to computer application to text. Like data processing by the computer, it also processes words or text. Word processing is another major application of computer to create, view, edit store, retrieve and finally print text materials. The modern electronic offices have been using automated and centralised typing, dictation, copying, and filing information. A device which do word processing naturally, such as composing, correspondence in format, editing, revising, etc. Optical character recognisition or fascimile equipment coverts printed materials into machine readable text. A text can be stored in memory. The Keyboard is the typewriter. Text editing process cover entering, editing, and deletion of text, and printing process function includes to print, read. Computer technology is now greatly used in modern offices to transmit ideas, facts etc., into written communication. The process avoids labourious typing or to cyclostyle or print the letters. When a number of letters are to be sent to customers, it is possible to personalise each letter by printing on the word processor printer for each address. The matter can be stored in magnetic storage device, and be used to send a similar letter. The advantages of word processing are easy correction, revision, storage of message, easy creation of new documents from stored data, no erasures, overtyping on white paper as it is the case in the case of typewriter; print charts the figures, faster and efficient than mechanical typewriters, goodwill and satisfaction of the customers. Processing is a manipulation of words. The input is through keyboard and the output may be produced on either a display screen or a printer. The common types of business communications are repetitive letters, standard documents, special reports and financial reports. The basic functions in all business communication are Input processing, storage and output. Keyboard is the input component, processing unit receives instructions, coordinates the entire system, storage is a memory component receives and stores data or text for manipulation. The output may be obtained either on the screen of video display or a printer. There are many organisations today which have introduced communications technology to reduce cost, avoid delay, achieve accuracy and speed. A word processing package is used to create, view, edit, store, retrieve and print matter. Use of computer in word processing application is more important in electronic office.

**Information and Communication Network**

New communication technologies are helping in building up national and international information Communication Networks and a new information order is getting developed. The network has great capacity of storing, processing and transmitting information electronically, and any one having access to the network can receive any information from anywhere stored in the network. Versatility and capabilities of the network are expanding with unimaginable rapidity. With the fifth generation computers round the corner, and such technological change in the offing, in which TV electronic tube may be replaced by liquid crystal screens thereby reducing the size and cost of the television and increasing its portability and convenience, and the availability of more versatile satellites that would offer large number of channels and would link any two locations on the surface of the earth, the stage is well set for revolutionary changes, which even the best experts in the field fear to forecast. The new information technologies have, on the whole, very specialised and centralised needs for the development of their hardware. However, its mass production has made the product very economical. Further, the software developments, appropriate to local situations and requirements, necessary to use new technologies have given the technologies, the common features of being economical, versatile, having wider accessibility and decentralised nature.

The new communication technologies, with the above characteristics, will generate creative processes and activities at various localities and will effectively contribute to the creation of knowledge, which itself will become decentralised in future.

Broadcasting (radio, television) and non-broadcasting (audio and video cassettes, computers, etc.) channels of communication network offer an excellent opportunity of creating an Educational Network. The educational network will essentially consist of storage of learning material in audio-visual and textual forms linkages through terminals with the receiver.

The recent information technology revolution has transformed a communication-conscious human society into, metaphorically speaking, an information obsessed global village in the short span of just two decades. The course of development for the developing and the underdeveloped countries is no longer linear-sequential; it is increasingly characterised by leap-fogging wherein one or more stages are bypassed in order to arrive at the state-of-art stage of information technology. Today, our traditional concepts of 'knowledge' and 'information' call for re-examination. "Knowledge is power" is the slogan of this decade. Distance has been whisked away, thanks largely to information technology. For the first time in human history, people from different parts of this plannet can talk to see one another and be simultaneously watched by millions of viewers all over the world. Tele-conferencing no longer belongs to the world of science fiction it is a reality on our national TV network. At present, our children face an incessant "information blitzkreig." India never had such generation of knowledgeable youngsters who quite often know a lot more than their parents. Information technology has come to stay whether we want it or not and its implications in terms of accelerated socialisation and learning are quite fascinating, sometimes even ominous. The only option available to us is to ride this tigress of information technology and our skill lies in riding it to our advantage. "Knowledge and information" constitute the meeting-point between education and information technology.

If we understand the range of possibilities available to us through information technology, we may be able to understand better some of the constraints that have characterised educational endeavour throughout human history and which have circumscribed its range as well as effectiveness. Like its mother 'science', 'information technology' may prove 'a faithful servant or a fiendish master' depending on how judiciously and to what purpose we successfully master it. Consequently, there is a need greater than ever before to perceive the entire gamut of possible relationship between information technology and education so that the former is made subservient to our needs.

Information experts now make a distinction between information and knowledge. Knowledge, consequently, is no longer the same as information. Information comprises data transformed into a meaningful guide for specific action. Knowledge, on the other hand, is an organised body of information that facilitates insights and judgments. To quote Stonier, "what is information at one level may be data at the next." Thus facts, data, information and knowledge constitute a hierarchical order. One of the imperceptible shifts in our social order relates to the fact that political power has increasingly become information-based; till the recent past, it was capital-based. Hence, information and knowledge are the grist common to the mills of education as well as to information technology. Information Technology (IT) has meant different things to different persons.

However, the consensus of opinion is more inclined to define IT as the technology that deals with "the collection, storage, processing, dissemination and use of information" or "new ways of storing, processing, and transmitting information brought about by rapid developments in electronics, computing and telecommunications." UNESCO has defined IT as comprising "the Scientific" technological and engineering disciplines and the management of techniques used in information handling and processing, their applications; computers and their interaction with men and machines; and associated social, economic and cultural matters." Thus IT is not entirely concerned with information processing hardware and software it has to be equally concerned with the fall-out that it generates in man's social, economic an cultural lie. Distinguishing among terms like technology (i.e., total body of knowledge pertinent to the generation and innovation of tools, machines and systems), artifacts (i.e., the interface between human beings and their environment enabling them to bridge the gap between their native insufficiencies and demanding and complex millieu), coping (i.e., the manipulation of three essential resources—matter, energy and information) and manipulation (i.e., various processes encompassing producing, processing, storing transmitting and consulting) as various aspects of IT. Hamelink defines IT as "the aggregate of scientific/technical disciplines basic to the product of devices (tools/machines) and systems for the capture, transportation, storage, processing and retrieval of voice, text, numerical and pictorial information."

Contrary to popular belief, IT has three forms, viz., primitive, intermediate and super also called low IT, mid IT and Hi-IT. IT provides the essential infrastructure for an unprecedented variety of human activities due to increased significance of resource information in various fields. Its effects are not limited to a section of society; it influences all people at all times. It has been hypothesised that "the most advanced stage of information society will be high mass knowledge creation society. The spirit of the information society will be the spirit of globalism, a symbiosis in which man and nature can live together in harmony, consisting, ethically of strict self-discipline and social contribution."

Education has all along been an activity related to a very sensitive area of human relationship—the development of children. Transmission of knowledge and information have been central to educational endeavour throughout its history. Expert and lay opinion might have differed about other purposes of education but so far as transmission of knowledge and information is concerned, they have been almost unanimous. Educational systems have always been expected to enable its consumer learners to acquire maximum knowledge and information in minimum time to promote the simultaneous progress of the individual an society. Education has occasionally been described as 'the knowledge industry.'

In fact, 'quality' may be defined as "conformance to the requirements or specifications". A more formal definition would be "the totality of features and characteristics of a product or service that bear on its ability to satisfy given needs. The achievement of quality requirements, as laid down by the customer, must be primary concern of any company, which should ensure that the quality desired is designed, built and maintained into its products at all stages of production, providing full satisfaction of the customer's expectations. In every organisation, the company should strive to make everyone of its employees feel that quality is a collective responsibility and each one has a definite role to play in achieving and maintaining the quality.

Quality assurance relates to the steps to be taken to determine and maintain the quality during manufacture which will make the product fit for the purpose intended in terms of its performance, cost and delivery time. Adequate controls are to be exercised on the quality in various phases right from the design and followed up till the product has been delivered and put into regular service. A holistic or 'total' approach, where everyone feels his responsibility to achieve the quality is termed Total Quality Control'.

The essential stages in a total quality control system would be (i) to set quality standards; (ii) to plan to achieve the specified quality utilising the available technological, manpower and material resources; (iii) to plan inspection and shop floor quality control; (iv) to manufacture right first time; (v) to correct any short comings in quality, if observed and finally, (vi) to provide for a long term quality control system with appropriate feed backs.

In order to achieve the requirements of quality, meeting with the expectations of customer and also to protect the interest of the company in terms of optimum cost for the desired quality, every company should develop and implement an information management system tailor-made to suit its needs. Such a system should be designed to perform the following major tasks:

1. Spell out clearly and broadly the management policy on quality for the guidance of all concerned, and provide a better understanding and appreciation of the same.
2. Help in building customer's confidence in the quality and reliability of the products.
3. Serve as a reference guide for all concerned in order to understand their role and responsibilities.
4. Have better understanding with suppliers and make them clear about the vendor control system.
5. Provide a reference for quality audit purpose.
6. Educate all the employees for clear understanding of the role and working of quality assurance department.

It is necessary to identify the activities contributing to quality, either directly or indirectly and then to define the responsibility and authority as regards quality for each activity, following up with providing coordination measures amongst different activities.

It is further essential in a well-designed quality management system to identify the needs for training of personnel at various levels, such as, workers, production supervisors, technical personnel connected with quality assurance, design staff, executive and managerial personnel, all of whom have a role to play in achieving and maintaining quality. The arrangements to be made or methods employed to provide training should also be established.

It goes without saying that whatever means are adopted or policies laid down, quality control cannot be achieved on a continuous basis without full cooperation and involvement of people. Workers attitude directly mirrors the management's competence and structure.

According to Peter Drucker, whether a business enterprise performs, depends in the final analysis on its ability to get people to perform. Appropriate means of motivation and worker participation, including organisation of quality circles should be established and follow-up action provided in the quality management system.

It is the customer who determines the business. Any quality system therefore, must be customer-oriented. Accordingly, it is imperative that due importance is given to market potential, market trends and customer relations.

## REFERENCES

Alfred, R.E., Quality Costs-where to start, *Quality* 18, (8, 9 and 10) Aug., Sept., Oct. 1979.

Antoni; *Learning at a Distance: A World Perspective,* p. 290.

Brewer, CE., et al, "Managing the company-wide quality Manual", *Quality,* 22, (6) June 1983.

Chartrand, R.L. and Morentz; J.W., *Information Technology Serving Society,* London, Pergamon, 1979.

Donald H. Sanders: *Computer Concepts and Applications,* Mcgraw Hill International Editions, 1987, p. 533.

Donald H. Sanders: *Computer Concepts and Applications,* McGraw-hill International Editions. Computer Science Series, 1987, p. 14.

Feigenbaum, A.V., *Total Quality Control,* McGraw Hill, 1983.

G.A. Yewdall and others, *Management Information,* Pan Books Ltd., London, 1971, p. 242.

Gough, J.E. and R.J. Mcdonald (1981), "Audio Cassettes as an Educational Medium in Distance Educatior", Paper presented to RSDTA, Penang (Malaysia). Quoted in *Studies in Distance Education,* Association of Indian Universities, Indira Gandhi National Open University, New Delhi, 1988, pp. 102-103.

Griffin, C.C.M. (1981), "Moral Ties and Satellite Networks: Creating 'Community' for Distance Learning Across Cultures of the South Pacific", paper presented to RSDTA, Penang (Malaysia).

Grove, Michael, (1984), "The Interactive Videodisc in Education and Training." In osborne, C.W. (Ed.) 1984, International Yearbook of Educational Technology 1984-85. London, Kogan page.

Gwynn, Robin (1981), "Tutorials without a Tutor: Encouraging student-student contract at a Distance", a Sena Forum Papers. As Quoted in *Studies in Distance Education.* Association of Indian Universities,, Indira Gandhi National Open University, New Delhi, 1988, p. 103.

Hamelink, C.J.: *Information Technology and The Third World,* A paper presented at XV IAMCR Conference on 26th Aug. 1986 at New Delhi, p. 2.

Hussain and Hussain: *Information Processing Systems for Management,* Richard D. Irwin. Inc., Homewood, Illinois, Irwin-Dorsey Ltd., Georgetown, Ontario, 1981, p. 24.

Jain, P.L., *Principles of Foundry Technology,* Tata McGraw Hill, 1986 (2nd Ed.).

Masuda, Yoneji; *The Information Society As Post-Industrial Society,* Tokyo, Institute for the Information Society, 1980, p. 33.

Myers and Myers: *Managing by Communication: An Organisational Approach,* McGraw Hill International Book Company, 1982, p. 15.

*New Technologies in Higher Education,* Association of Indian Universities, 1986, p. 51.

Ott, Ellis R., "Process improvement with quality control", *Quality,* April, 1980.

Potter, Geoff (1981), "Satellite-based Distance Education: Problems and Solutions", paper presented to RSDTA, Penang (Malaysia).

Stonier, T., *The Wealth of Information,* London, Thames Methuen, 1983, p. 19.

Wadworth H.M. et al., *Modern Methods for Quality Control and Improvement,* John Wiley; 1986.

# Appendix

## NEW TELECOM POLICY, 1999

*The following is the full text of the New Telecom Policy 1999 announced here today:*

### 1.1 Importance of Telecommunications

The Government of India (Government) recognises that provision of world class telecommunications infrastructure and information is the key to rapid economic and social development of the country.

It is critical not only for the development of the Information Technology industry, but also has widespread ramifications on the entire economy of the country. It is also anticipated that going forward, a major part of the GDP of the country would be contributed by this sector. Accordingly, it is of vital importance to the country that there be a comprehensive and forward looking telecommunications policy which creates an enabling framework for development of this industry.

### 1.2 NTP 1994—Objectives and Achievements

In 1994, the Government announced the National Telecom Policy which defined certain important objectives, including availability of telephone on demand, provision of world class services at reasonable prices, ensuring India's emergence as major manufacturing / export base of telecom equipment and universal availability of basic telecom services to all villages. It also announced a series of specific targets to be achieved by 1997.

As against the NTP 1994 target of provision of 1 PCO per 500 urban population and coverage of all 6 lac villages, DoT has achieved an urban PCO penetration of 1 PCO per 522 and has been able to provide telephone coverage to only 3.1 lac villages. As regards provision of total telephone lines in the country, DoT has provided 8.73 million telephone lines against the eighth plan target of 7.5 million lines.

NTP 1994 also recognised that the required resources for achieving these targets would not be available only out of Government sources and concluded that private investment and involvement of the private sector was required to bridge the resource gap. The Government invited private sector participation in a phased manner from the early nineties, initially for value added services such as Paging Services and Cellular Mobile Telephone Services (CMTS) and thereafter for Fixed Telephone Services (FTS).

After a competitive bidding process, licenses were awarded to 8 CMTS operators in the four metros, 14 CMTS operators in 18 state circles, 6 BTS operators in 6 state circles and to paging operators in 27 cities and 18 state circles. VSAT services were liberalised for providing data services to closed user groups. Licences were issued to 14 operators in the private sector out of which only nine licencees are operational.

The Government has recently announced the policy for Internet Service Provision (ISP) by private operators and has commenced licensing of the same. The Government has also announced opening up of Global Mobile Personal Communications by Satellite (GMPCS) and has issued one provisional license. Issue of licenses to other prospective GMPCS operators is under consideration.

The Government recognises that the result of the

privatisation has so far not been entirely satisfactory. While there has been a rapid rollout of cellular mobile networks in the metros and states with currently over 1 million subscribers, most of the projects today are facing problems. The main reason, according to the cellular and basic operators, has been the fact that the actual revenues realised by these projects have been far short of the projections and the operators are unable to arrange financing for their projects and therefore complete their projects. Basic telecom services by private operators have only just commenced in a limited way in two of the six circles where licenses were awarded. As a result, some of the targets as envisaged in the objectives of the NTP 1994 have remained unfulfilled. The private sector entry has been slower than what was envisaged in the NTP 1994. The government views the above developments with concern as it would adversely affect the further development of the sector and recognises the need to take a fresh look at the policy framework for this sector.

### 1.3 Need for a New Telecom Policy

In addition to some of the objectives of NTP 1994 not being fulfilled, there have also been far reaching developments in the recent past in the telecom, IT, consumer electronics and media industries world-wide. Convergence of both markets and technologies is a reality that is forcing realignment of the industry. At one level, telephone and broadcasting industries are entering each other's markets, while at another level, technology is blurring the difference between different conduit systems such as wireline and wireless.

As in the case of most countries, separate licences have been issued in our country for basic, cellular, ISP, satellite and cable TV operators each with separate industry structure, terms of entry and varying requirement to create infrastructure. However this convergence now allows operators to use their facilities to deliver some services reserved for other operators, necessitating a relook into the existing policy framework. The new telecom policy framework is also required to facilitate India's vision of becoming an IT superpower and develop a world class telecom infrastructure in the country.

**2.0 Objectives and targets of the New Telecom Policy 1999 The objectives of the NTP 1999 are as under:**

Access to telecommunications is of utmost importance for achievement of the country's social and economic goals. Availability of affordable and effective communications for the citizens is at the core of the vision and goal of the telecom policy.

Strive to provide a balance between the provision of universal service to all uncovered areas, including the rural areas, and the provision of high-level services capable of meeting the needs of the country's economy; Encourage development of telecommunication facilities in remote, hilly and tribal areas of the country; Create a modern and efficient telecommunications infrastructure taking into account the convergence of IT, media, telecom and consumer electronics and thereby propel India into becoming an IT superpower; Convert PCO's, wherever justified, into Public Teleinfo centres having multimedia capability like ISDN services, remote database access, government and community information systems etc.

Transform in a time bound manner, the telecommunications sector to a greater competitive environment in both urban and rural areas providing equal opportunities and level playing field for all players; Strengthen research and development efforts in the country and provide an impetus to build world-class manufacturing capabilities. Achieve efficiency and transparency in spectrum management. Protect defence and security interests of the country. Enable Indian Telecom Companies to become truly global players.

In line with the above objectives, the specific targets that the NTP 1999 seeks to achieve would be:

Make available telephone on demand by the year 2002 and sustain it thereafter so as to achieve a teledensity of 7 by the year 2005 and 15 by the year 2010 Encourage development of telecom in rural areas making it more affordable by suitable tariff structure and making rural communication mandatory for all fixed service providers Increase rural teledensity from the current level of 0.4 to 4 by the year 2010 and provide reliable transmission media in all rural areas Achieve telecom coverage of all villages in the country and provide reliable media to all exchanges by the year 2002 Provide Internet access to all district head quarters by the year 2000 Provide high speed data and multimedia capability using technologies including ISDN to all towns with a population greater than 2 lac by the year 2002

**3.0 New Policy Framework**

The New Policy Framework must focus on creating an environment, which enables continued attraction of investment in the sector and allows creation of communication infrastructure by leveraging on technological development. Towards this end, the New Policy Framework would look at the telecom service sector as follows – Cellular Mobile Service Providers, Fixed Service Providers and Cable

Service Providers, collectively referred to as 'Access Providers' Radio Paging Service Providers Public Mobile Radio Trunking Service Providers National Long Distance Operators International Long Distance Operators Other Service Providers Global Mobile Personal Communication by Satellite (GMPCS) Service Providers V-SAT based Service Providers

### 3.1 Access Providers

#### *3.1.1 Cellular Mobile Service Providers*

The Cellular Mobile Service Providers (CMSP) shall be permitted to provide mobile telephony services including permission to carry its own long distance traffic within their service area without seeking an additional licence. Direct interconnectivity between licenced CMSP's and any other type of service provider (including another CMSP) in their area of operation including sharing of infrastructure with any other type of service provider shall be permitted. Interconnectivity between service providers in different service areas shall be reviewed in consultation with TRAI and the same would be announced by August 15, 1999 as a part of the structure for opening up national long distance. The CMSP shall be allowed to directly interconnect with the VSNL after opening of national long distance from January 1, 2000. The CMSP shall be free to provide, in its service area of operation, all types of mobile services including voice and non-voice messages, data services and PCOs utilising any type of network equipment, including circuit and/or packet switches, that meet the relevant International Telecommunication Union (ITU) / Telecommunication Engineering Center (TEC) standards.

CMSP would be granted separate licence, for each service area. Licences would be awarded for an initial period of twenty years and would be extendible by additional periods of ten years thereafter. For this purpose, service areas would be categorised into the four metro circles and Telecom circles as per the existing policy. CMSP would be eligible to obtain licences for any number of service areas.

Availability of adequate frequency spectrum is essential not only for providing optimal bandwidth to every operator but also for entry of additional operators. Based on the immediately available frequency spectrum band, apart from the two private operators already licenced, DOT / MTNL would be licenced to be the third operator in each service area in case they want to enter, in a time bound manner. In order to ensure level playing field between different service providers in similar situations, licence fee would be payable by DoT also. However, as DoT is the national service provider having immense rural and social obligations, the Government will reimburse full licence fee to the DoT.

It is proposed to review the spectrum utilisation from time to time keeping in view the emerging scenario of spectrum availability, optimal use of spectrum, requirements of market, competition and other interest of public. The entry of more operators in a service area shall be based on the recommendation of the TRAI who will review this as required and no later than every two years. CMSP operators would be required to pay a one time entry fee. The basis for determining the entry fee and the basis for selection of additional operators would be recommended by the TRAI.

Apart from the one time entry fee, CMSP operators would also be required to pay licence fee based on a revenue share. It is proposed that the appropriate level of entry fee and percentage of revenue share arrangement for different service areas would be recommended by TRAI in a time-bound manner, keeping in view the objectives of the New Telecom Policy.

### *3.1.2 Fixed Service Providers*

The Fixed Service Providers (FSP) shall be freely permitted to establish 'last mile' linkages to provide fixed services and carry long distance traffic within their service area without seeking an additional licence. Direct interconnectivity between FSP's and any other type of service provider (including another FSP) in their area of operation and sharing of infrastructure with any other type of service provider shall be permitted. Interconnectivity between service providers in different service areas shall be reviewed in consultation with TRAI and the same would be announced by August 15, 1999 as a part of the structure for opening up of national long distance. The FSP shall be allowed to directly interconnect with the VSNL after the opening up of national long distance from January 1, 2000.

The FSP may also utilise last mile linkages or transmission links within its service area made available by other service providers. The FSP shall be free to provide, in his service area of operation, all types of fixed services including voice and non-voice messages and data services, utilising any type of network equipment, including circuit and/or packet switches, that meet the relevant International Telecommunication Union (ITU) / Telecommunication Engineering Center (TEC) standards.

The FSP shall be granted separate licence, on a non-exclusive basis, for each service area of operation. Licences would be awarded for an initial period of twenty years which shall be extended by additional periods of ten years thereafter. The FSPs shall be eligible to obtain licences for any number of service areas. While market forces will ultimately determine the number of fixed service providers, during transition, number of entrants have to be carefully decided to eliminate non-serious players and allow new entrants to establish themselves.

Therefore, the option of entry of multiple operators for a period of five years for the service areas where no licences have been issued is adopted. The number of players and their mode of selection will be recommended by TRAI in a time-bound manner. The FSP licencees would be required to pay a one time entry fee. All FSP licencees shall pay licence fee in the form of a revenue share.

It is proposed that the appropriate level of entry fee and percentage of revenue share and basis for selection of new operators for different service areas of operation would be recommended by TRAI in a time-bound manner, keeping in view the objectives of the New Telecom Policy. As in the case for cellular, for WLL also, availability of appropriate frequency spectrum as required is essential not only for providing optimal bandwidth to every operator but also for entry of additional operators. It is proposed to review the spectrum utilisation from time to time keeping in view the emerging scenario of spectrum availability, optimal use of spectrum, requirements of market, competition and other interest of public.

The WLL frequency shall be awarded to the FSPs requiring the same, based on the payment of an additional one time fee over and above the FSP entry fee. The basis for determining the entry fee and the basis for assigning WLL frequency shall be recommended by the TRAI. All FSP operators utilising WLL shall pay a licence fee in the form of a revenue share for spectrum utilization. This percentage of revenue share shall be over and above the percentage payable for the FSP licence.

It is proposed that the appropriate level of entry fee and percentage of revenue share for WLL for different service areas of operation will be recommended by TRAI in a time-bound manner, keeping in view the objectives of the New Telecom Policy.

### *3.1.3 Cable Service Providers*

Under the provisions of the Cable Regulation Act, 1995, Cable Service Providers (CSP) shall continue to be freely permitted to provide 'last mile' linkages and switched services within their service areas of operation and operate media services, which are essentially one-way, entertainment related services.

Direct interconnectivity between CSP's and any other type of service provider in their area of operation and sharing of infrastructure with any other type of service provider shall be permitted. Interconnectivity between service providers in different service areas shall be reviewed in consultation with TRAI and the same would be announced by August 15, 1999 as a part of the structure for opening up national long distance. In view of convergence, it is highly likely that two-way communication (including voice, data and information services) through cable network would emerge in a significant way in future. Offering of these services through the cable network would tantamount to providing fixed services.

Accordingly, in case the above two-way communication services are to be provided by CSPs utilising their network, they would also be required to obtain an FSP licence and be bound by the licence conditions of the FSPs, with a view to ensure level playing field. 3.2 Internet Telephony Internet telephony shall not be permitted at this stage. However, Government will continue to monitor the technological innovations and their impact on national development and review this issue at an appropriate time.

### 3.3 Radio Paging Service Providers

The Radio Paging Service Providers (RPSP) shall be permitted to provide paging services within their service area of operation. Direct interconnectivity between licenced RPSPs and any other type of service provider in their area of operation including sharing of infrastructure shall be permitted. Interconnectivity between service providers in different service areas shall be reviewed in consultation with TRAI and the same would be announced by August 15, 1999 as a part of the structure for opening up of national long distance.

The RPSP shall be granted separate licence, on a non-exclusive basis, for each service area of operation. Licences would be awarded for an initial period of twenty years and will be extended by additional periods of ten years thereafter.

For this purpose, the service areas would be categorised as per the existing structure. The RPSP shall be eligible to obtain licences for any number of service areas. Availability of adequate radio frequency spectrum is essential not only for providing optimal bandwidth to every operator but also for entry of additional operators.

It is proposed to review the spectrum utilisation from time to time keeping in view the emerging scenario of spectrum availability, optimal use of spectrum, requirements of market, competition and other interest of public. The entry of more operators in a service area shall be based on the recommendation of the TRAI who would review this as required and no later than every two years..

The radio paging licencees shall pay a one time entry

fee. The basis for determining the entry fee and the basis for selection of additional operators will be recommended by the TRAI. All radio paging licencees shall pay licence fee as a revenue share. It is proposed that the appropriate level of entry fee and percentage of revenue share for different service areas of operation will be recommended by TRAI in a time-bound manner, keeping in view the objectives of the New Telecom Policy. Further, TRAI may also examine and recommend the revenue sharing arrangements between RPSP and other access providers, subject to technical feasibility.

**3.4 Public Mobile Radio Trunking Service Providers**

The Public Mobile Radio Trunking Service Providers (PMRTSP) shall be permitted to provide mobile radio trunking services within their service area of operation. Direct interconnectivity between licenced PMRTSP's and any other type of service provider in their area of operation shall be permitted after examining the legal implications in view of the CMSP licences The PMRTSP shall be granted separate licence, on a non-exclusive basis, for each service area of operation. Licences would be awarded for an initial period of twenty years and will be extended by additional periods of ten years thereafter.

For this purpose, the service areas would be categorised as per the existing structure. The PMRTSP shall be eligible to obtain licences for any number of service areas. PMRTSP licencees would be required to pay a one time entry fee. The basis for determining the entry fee and the basis for selection of additional operators will be recommended by the TRAI. Apart from the one time entry fee, PMRTSP licencees would also be required to pay licence fee based on a revenue share. It is proposed that the appropriate level of entry fee and percentage of revenue share arrangement for different service areas would be recommended by TRAI in a time-bound manner, keeping in view the objectives of the New Telecom Policy.

**3.5 National Long Distance Operator**

National long distance service beyond service area to the private operators will be opened for competition with effect from January 1, 2000. To promote setting up long distance bandwidth capacity in the country, provide a choice to consumers and promote competition, all NLDOs should be able to access subscribers. With a view to achieve the above, all access providers shall be mandatorily required to provide interconnection to the NLDOs resulting in choice for subscribers to make long distance calls through any operator.

For this purpose, the terms and conditions and other modalities would be worked out in consultation with TRAI and the same will be announced by August 15, 1999. The terms and conditions would also specify the number of operators, licence conditions on revenue sharing basis and other related issues. Usage of the existing backbone network of public and private power transmission companies / Railways / GAIL, ONGC etc. shall be allowed immediately for national long distance data communication and from January 1, 2000 for national long distance voice communications. Resale would be permitted for domestic telephony, announcement for the modalities thereof to be announced alongwith the opening up of national long distance by August 15, 1999. Resale on international long distance will not be permitted till the year 2004.

**3.6 International Long Distance Services**

The subject of opening up of international telephony service to competition will be reviewed by the year 2004.

### 3.7 Other Service Providers

For applications like tele-banking, tele-medicine, tele-education, tele-trading, e-commerce, other service providers will be allowed to operate by using infrastructure provided by various access providers. No licence fee will be charged but registration for specific services being offered will be required. These service providers will not infringe on the jurisdiction of other access providers and they will not provide switched telephony.

### 3.8 Global Mobile Personal Communication Services

The Government has opened up the GMPCS market in India and has issued a provisional licence. The terms of the final licence would need to be finalised in consultation with TRAI by June 30, 1999. All the calls originating or terminating in India shall pass through VSNL gateway or in case of bypass, it should be possible to monitor these calls in the Indian gateways. VSNL is also to be compensated in case gateway is bypassed.

The GMPCS operators shall be free to provide voice and non-voice messages, data service and information services utilising any type of network equipment, including circuit and/or packet switches that meet the relevant International Telecommunication Union (ITU) / Telecommunication Engineering Center (TEC) standards. However, the licences be awarded after the proposals are scrutinised from the security angle by the Government. The appropriate entry fee/revenue sharing structure would be recommended by TRAI, keeping in view the objectives of the New Telecom Policy.

### 3.9 SATCOM Policy

The SATCOM Policy shall provide for users to avail of transponder capacity from both domestic / foreign satellites.

However, the same has to be in consultation with the Department of Space. Under the existing ISP policy, international long distance communication for data has been opened up. The gateways for this purpose shall be allowed to use SATCOM. It has also been decided that Ku frequency band shall be allowed to be used for communication purposes.

### *3.9.1 VSAT Service Providers*

The VSAT Service Providers shall be granted separate licence, on a non-exclusive basis for an initial period of twenty years and will be extended by additional periods of ten years thereafter. Interconnectivity between service providers in different service areas shall be reviewed in consultation with TRAI and the same would be announced as a part of the structure for opening up national long distance by August 15, 1999. The VSAT service providers shall be granted separate licence, on a non-exclusive basis. Licences would be awarded for an initial period of twenty years and will be extended by additional periods of ten years thereafter.

VSAT licencees would be required to pay a one time entry fee. The basis for determining the entry fee and the basis for selection of additional operators will be recommended by the TRAI. Apart from the one time entry fee, VSAT licencees would also be required to pay licence fee based on a revenue share. It is proposed that the appropriate level of entry fee and percentage of revenue share arrangement would be recommended by TRAI in a time-bound manner, keeping in view the objectives of the New Telecom Policy.

### 3.10 Electronic Commerce

On line Electronic Commerce will be encouraged so

that information can be passed seamlessly. The requirement to develop adequate bandwidth of the order of 10 GB on national routes and even terrabits on certain congested important national routes will be immediately addressed to so that growth of IT as well as electronic commerce will not be hampered.

**3.11 Resolution of Problems of Existing Operators**

The New Policy Framework which seeks to significantly redefine the competitive nature of industry, would be applicable to new licensees. There are, however, multiple licences that have been issued by the Government for cellular mobile services, basic services, radio paging services, internet services etc. It is the Government's intention to satisfactorily resolve the problems being faced by existing operators in a manner which is consistent with their contractual obligations and is legally tenable.

**4.0 Restructuring of DoT**

World-wide, the incumbent, usually the Government owned operator plays a major role in the development of the telecom sector. In India, DoT is responsible for the impressive growth in number of lines from 58.1 lakh on April 1, 1992 to 191 lakh in December 1998, showing a CAGR of 20%. DoT is expected to continue to play an important, and indeed, dominant role in the development of the sector. Currently, the licensing, policy making and the service provision functions are under a single authority. The Government has decided to separate the policy and licensing functions of DoT from the service provision functions as a precursor to corporatisation. The corporatisation of DoT shall be done keeping in mind the interests of all stakeholders by the year 2001. All the future relationship (competition, resource raising etc.) of

MTNL / VSNL with the corporatised DoT would be based on best commercial principles.

The synergy of MTNL, VSNL and the coporatised DoT would be utilised to open up new vistas for operations in other countries.

**5.0 Spectrum Management**

With the proliferation of new technologies and the growing demand for telecommunication services, the demand on spectrum has increased manifold. It is, therefore, essential that spectrum be utilised efficiently, economically, rationally and optimally.

There is a need for a transparent process of allocation of frequency spectrum for use by a service and making it available to various users under specific conditions. The National Frequency Allocation Plan (NFAP) was last established in 1981, and has been modified from time to time since. With the proliferation of new technologies it is essential to revise the NFAP in its entirety so that it could become the basis for development, manufacturing and spectrum utilization activities in the country amongst all users.

The NFAP is presently under review and the revised NFAP-2000 would be made public by the end of 1999, detailing information regarding allocation of frequency bands for various services, without including security information. NFAP shall be reviewed no later than every two years and shall be in line with radio regulations of International Telecommunication Union. Relocation of existing Spectrum and Compensation: Considering the growing need of spectrum for communication services, there is a need to make adequate spectrum available Appropriate frequency bands have historically been assigned to defence & others and efforts would be made towards relocating them so as to have optimal utilisation of spectrum. Compensation for relocation may be provided out of spectrum fee and revenue share levied by Government. There is a need to review the spectrum allocations in a planned manner so that required frequency bands are available to the service providers. There is a need to have a transparent process of allocation of frequency spectrum which is effective and efficient. This would be examined further in the light of ITU guidelines. For the present, the following course of action shall be adopted. Spectrum usage fee shall be charged. Setting up an empowered Inter-Ministerial Group to be called as Wireless Planning Coordination Committee (WPCC) as part of the Ministry of Communications for periodical review of spectrum availability and broad allocation policy. Massive computerisation in the WPC Wing will be started during the next three months' time so as to achieve the objective of making all operations completely computerised by the end of year 2000.

### 6.0 Universal Service Obligation

The Government is committed to provide access to all people for basic telecom services at affordable and reasonable prices. The Government seeks to achieve the following universal service objectives: Provide voice and low speed data service to the balance 2.9 lac uncovered villages in the country by the year 2002 Achieve Internet access to all district head quarters by the year 2000 Achieve telephone on demand in urban and rural areas by 2002 The resources for meeting the USO would be raised through a 'universal access levy' which would be a percentage of the revenue earned by all the operators under various licences. The percentage of revenue share towards universal access levy would be decided by the Government in consultation with TRAI. The implementation of the USO obligation for rural / remote areas would be undertaken by all fixed service providers who shall be reimbursed from the funds from the universal access levy. Other service providers shall also be encouraged to participate in USO provision subject to technical feasibility and shall be reimbursed from the funds from the universal access levy.

**7.0 Role of Regulator**

The Telecom Regulatory Authority of India (TRAI) was formed in January 1997 with a view to provide an effective regulatory framework and adequate safeguards to ensure fair competition and protection of consumer interests. The Government is committed to a strong and independent regulator with comprehensive powers and clear authority to effectively perform its functions. Towards this objective the following approach will be adopted: Section 13 of the TRAI Act gives adequate powers to TRAI to issue directions to service providers. Further, under Section 14 of the Act, the TRAI has full adjudicatory powers to resolve disputes between service providers. To ensure a level playing fields, it will be clarified that the TRAI has the powers to issue directions under Section 13 to Government (in its role as service provider) and further to adjudicate under Section 14 of the Act, all disputes arising between Government (in its role as service provider) and any other service provider. TRAI will be assigned the arbitration function for resolution of disputes between Government (in its role as licensor) and any licensee.

The Government will invariably seek TRAI's recommendations on the number and timing of new licences before taking decision on issue of new licenses in future. The functions of licensor and policy maker would continue to be discharged by Government in its sovereign capacity. In respect of functions where TRAI has been assigned a recommendatory role, it would not be statutorily mandatory for Government to seek TRAI's recommendations.

## 8.0 Other Issues

### *8.1 Standardisation*

To enable the establishment of an integrated telecommunication network, common standards with regard to equipment and services would be specified by the Telecom Engineering Centre (TEC).

TEC would also continue to grant interconnect and interface approvals for various service providers.

### *8.2 Telecom Equipment Manufacture*

With a view to promoting indigenous telecom equipment manufacture for both domestic use and export, the Government would provide the necessary support and encouragement to the sector, including suitable incentives to the service providers utilising indigenous equipment.

### *8.3 Human Resource Development and Training*

Human resources are considered more vital than physical resources. Emphasis would be placed on the development of human resources for all fields related to telecommunications and the dispersal of this expertise to the related fields. Such expertise shall also be made available to other countries.

### *8.4 Telecom Research and Development*

Recognising that telecommunications is a prime pre-requisite for the development of other technologies, telecommunications research and development (R&D) activities would be encouraged.

Government would take steps to ensure that the industry invests adequately in R&D for service provision as well as manufacturing. Indigenous R&D would be actively encouraged with a view to accelerate local industrial growth and hasten transfer of technology. Premier technical institutions would be encouraged to undertake R&D activities on a contribution basis by the telecom service providers and manufacturers so as to develop multi-dimensional R&D activities in telecommunications and information technology.

### *8.5 Disaster Management*

International co-operation in the use of terrestrial and satellite telecommunications technologies in the prediction, monitoring and early warning of disasters, especially in the early dissemination of information would be encouraged. Financial commitment to disaster management telephony and the development of appropriate regulatory framework for unhindered use of trans-boundary telecommunications would be put in place.

### *8.6 Remote Area Telephony*

Rural Telephony, areas of North East, Jammu & Kashmir and other hilly areas, tribal blocks, etc. may be identified as a special thrust areas for accelerated development of telecommunications. The Ministry of Defence shall be assigned a more active role in the development of telecommunications in such remote areas as are identified for accelerated development of telecommunications.

### *8.7 Export of Telecom Equipment and Services*

Export of telecom equipment and services would be actively incentivised. Synergies among the various telecom players (manufacturers and service providers) would be exploited and used to provide integrated solutions for exports.

### *8.8 Right of Way*

Government recognises that expeditious approvals for right-of-way clearances to all service providers are critical for timely implementation of telecom networks. The Central / State Government / Local bodies / Ministry of Surface Transport etc. shall take necessary steps to facilitate the same.

### 9.0 Changes in Legislation

The Indian telecommunications system continues to be governed by the provisions of the Indian Telegraph Act, 1885 (ITA 1885) and the Indian Wireless Act, 1933. Substantial changes have taken place in the telecommunications sector since 1992. ITA 1885 needs to be replaced with a more forward looking Act.

# Glossary

**Acculturation**: In a media context, the tendency of reporters or other media professionals to adopt the ideas and attitudes of the groups they cover or with which they have a great deal of contact.

**Advertising agency**: A company that handles both the creative and the business side of an advertising campaign for its clients.

**Agencies of socialization**: The various people or organizations that contribute to the socialization of an individual.

**Agency**: Organization that handles basic needs of advertisers.

**Alphabet**: A group of letters used to symbolize each of the sounds that make up a word.

**Arbitron**: The professional research organization that measures radio audiences.

**Audit Bureau of Circulations (ABC)**: An organization formed by advertisers and publishers in 1914 to establish ground rules for counting circulation data.

**Authoritarian theory**: The prevailing belief that a ruling elite should guide the intellectually inferior masses.

**Banner ads**: Type of advertising found on web pages.

**Beware surveillance**: A media function that occurs when the media inform the public of short-term, long-term, or chronic threats.

**Billboard**: The sound-recording industry trade publication that tabulates record popularity.

**Block booking**: A policy of major film studios that required theater owners to show several of a studio's low-quality films before they could receive the same studio's top-quality films.

**Broadband**: Increased bandwidth for Internet connections, which speeds up downloads.

**Browsers**: Type of software that lets individuals search for content on the World Wide Web.

**Business-to-business advertising**: Advertising directed not at the general public but at other businesses.

**Campaign**: In advertising, a large number of ads that stress the same theme and appear over a specified length of time.

**Carriage fee**: Fee paid by cable systems to carry a cable network.

**Categorical imperative**: Ethical principle that states people should behave as they would wish all others to behave.

**Catharsis**: A release of pent-up emotion or energy.

**Catharsis theory**: A theory that suggests viewing aggression will purge the viewer's aggressive feelings.

**Cease-and-desist order**: A Federal Trade Commission order notifying an advertiser that a certain practice violates the law; failure to comply with a cease-and-desist order can result in fines being levied against the advertiser.

**Channel**: The pathway by which a message travels from sender to receiver.

**Circulation**: The total number of copies of a publication delivered to newsstands, vending machines, and subscribers.

**Clock hour**: Radio format that specifies every element of the program.

**Commercial television**: Television programs broadcast by local stations whose income is derived from selling time on their facilities to advertisers.

**Communications Act of 1934**: Act of Congress creating the Federal Communications Commission.

**Communist theory**: Theory of the press that holds the media should promote the goals of the ruling political party.

**Comprehensive layout**: The finished model of a print ad.

**Computer-assisted reporting (CAR)**: Skills involved in using the Internet to aid reporting.

**Concept testing**: A type of feedback in which a one- or two-paragraph description for a new series is presented to a sample of viewers for their reactions.

**Consent order**: Federal Trade Commission order in which the advertiser agrees to halt a certain advertising practice without admitting any violation of the law.

**Consequence**: The importance or weightiness of a news story.

**Consumer advertising**: Advertising directed at the general public.

**Controlled circulation**: A type of circulation in which publications are sent free or distributed to a select readership, such as airline passengers or motel guests.

**Convergence**: The blending of communication technologies.

**Conversational currency**: Topic material presented by the media that provides a common ground for social conversations.

**Copy**: Headlines and message in an ad.

**Creative boutique**: Advertising organization that specializes in the creative side of advertising.

**Credibility**: The trust that the audience holds for media that perform surveillance functions.

**Critical/cultural approach**: Analytical technique that examines power relationships in society and focuses on meanings people find in texts.

**Crystallization**: The sharpening and elaboration of a vaguely held attitude or predisposition.

**Cultivation analysis**: An area of research that examines whether television and other media encourage perceptions of reality that are more consistent with media portrayals than with actuality.

**Cycle**: In all-news radio, the amount of time that elapses before the program order is repeated.

**Defamation**: The act of harming the reputation of another by publishing false information.

**Demo**: A demonstration tape used to sell a musical performer or group.

**Developmental journalism**: Type of journalism, practiced by many Third World countries, that stresses national goals and economic development.

**Developmental theory**: The assumption that government uses media to further national, economic, and social goals.

**Digital technology**: A system that encodes information-sound, text, data, video-into a series of on and off pulses that are usually denoted as zeros and ones.

**Digital television (DTV)**: Television signals consisting of binary signals that allow for improved picture quality.

**Digital videodisk (DVD)**: A disk that stores audio, movies, video, and graphics in digital format that is compatible with DVD players and home computers.

**Direct action**: An ad that contains a direct response item (such as a toll-free number) that allows advertisers to see results quickly.

**Direct broadcast satellite (DBS)**: A system in which a home TV set receives a signal directly from an orbiting satellite.

**Disintermediation**: The process of delivering a product or service directly to the consumer.

**Distribution system**: The actual cables that deliver the signals to subscribers.

**Distributors**: Sector of media industry that takes products from manufacturers and delivers them to retailers.

**Double feature**: Practice started by theaters in the 1930s of showing two feature films on the same bill.

**Dummy**: Rough version of a magazine that's used for planning how final version will look.

**Dysfunction**: Consequence that is undesirable from the point of view of the welfare of society.

**Editorial policies**: Guidelines the print media follow to persuade the public on certain issues or to achieve specific goals.

**Electronic news gathering (ENG)**: Producing and airing field reports using small, lightweight portable TV equipment.

**E-mail**: Electronic messages sent from computer to computer.

**Encoding**: The activity in the communication process by which thoughts and ideas from the source are translated into a form that may be perceived by the senses.

**Equal Opportunities rule**: Part of the Communications Act of 1934; Section 315 allows bona fide candidates for public office to gain access to a broadcast medium during political campaigns.

**Evaluation**: Research done to measure the effectiveness of an advertising or a public relations campaign.

**Fairness Doctrine**: Now defunct FCC doctrine that required broadcast stations to provide various points of view on a controversial issue.

**Federal Communications Commission (FCC)**: A regulatory agency, composed of five individuals appointed by the president, whose responsibilities include broadcast and wire regulation.

**Feedback**: The responses of the receiver that shape and alter subsequent messages from the source.

**Field experiment**: An experiment that is conducted in a natural setting as opposed to a laboratory.

**First Amendment**: The first amendment of the Bill of Rights, stating that Congress shall make no law abridging the freedom of speech, or of the press.

**Focus group**: A group of 10 to 15 people led by a moderator that discusses predetermined topics.

**Format**: Consistent programming designed to appeal to a certain segment of the audience.

**Formative research**: Advertising research done before developing a campaign.

**Format wheel**: Visual aid that helps radio programmers plan what events happen during a given time period.

**Framing**: The general way a news medium treats a topic.

**Franchise**: An exclusive right to operate a business in a given territory.

**Freedom of Information Act (FOIA)**: Law stating that every federal executive-branch agency must publish instructions on what methods a member of the public should follow to get information.

**Free-link exchange**: Web advertising technique in which one company exchanges free ad space with another.

**Free marketplace of ideas**: Press philosophy that endorses the free flow of information.

**Full-service agency**: An ad agency that handles all phases of advertising for its clients.

**Functional approach**: A methodology that holds something is best understood by examining how it is used.

**Gag rules**: Judicial orders that restrict trial participants from giving information to the media or that restrain media coverage of events that occur in court.

**Gatekeepers**: Individuals who decide whether a given message will be distributed by a mass medium.

**Golden mean**: Ethical principle that states moderation is the key to virtue.

**Gramophone**: A "talking machine" patented in 1887 by Emile Berliner that utilized a disk instead of a cylinder.

**Graphophone**: A recording device similar to the phonograph, but utilizing a wax cylinder rather than tinfoil.

**Hard news**: Timely stories with significance for many people.

**Head end**: The antenna and related equipment of the cable system that receives and processes distant television signals so that they can be sent to subscribers' homes.

**Heavy metal**: Counterculture musical trend of the 1960s-1970s, characterized by a vaguely threatening style and heavy use of amplification and electronic equipment.

**Hegemony**: Dominance of one entity over another.

**Hicklin rule**: A long-standing obscenity standard based upon whether a book or other item contains isolated passages that might deprave or corrupt the mind of the most susceptible person.

**House drop**: The section of the cable that connects the feeder cable to the subscriber's TV set.

**Human interest**: News value that emphasizes the emotional, bizarre, offbeat, or uplifting nature of a news story.

**Hypertext**: Digital navigational tool that links one electronic document to another.

**IBOC (in-band, on-channel)**: Digital radio broadcasting system that is also compatible with current analog radio.

**Ideology**: Particular set of beliefs or ideas.

**Independents**: Radio or TV stations unaffiliated with any network.

**Indirect action ad**: Advertisement that works over the long run to build a company's image.

**Information gathering**: Phase of a public relations campaign where pertinent data are collected.

**Injunction**: A court order that requires an individual to do something or to stop doing something.

**Instrumental surveillance**: A media function that occurs when the media transmit information that is useful and helpful in everyday life.

**Internet addiction**: Condition in which a person spends too much time on the Internet, cannot control his or her Internet use, and neglects social responsibilities to spend time online.

**Interpersonal communication**: A method of communication in which one person (or group) interacts with another person (or group) without the aid of a mechanical device.

**Investigative reports**: News reporting that requires extraordinary efforts to gather information about matters of public importance.

**Jazz**: A form of popular music that emerged during the Roaring Twenties and was noted for its spontaneity and disdain of convention.

**Jazz journalism**: Journalism of the Roaring Twenties that was characterized by a lively style and a richly illustrated tabloid format.

**Joint-operating agreement (JOA)**: An agreement, intended to preserve editorial competition, in which two newspapers merge their business and printing operations but maintain separate newsrooms.

**Joint venture**: Method of movie financing in which several companies pool resources to finance films.

**Kinetoscope**: The first practical motion picture camera and viewing device, developed by William Dickson in 1889.

**Libel**: Written defamation that tends to injure a person's reputation or good name or that diminishes the esteem, respect, or goodwill due a person.

**Libel per quod**: Written material that becomes libelous under certain circumstances.

**Libel per se**: Falsely written accusations (such as labeling a person a "thief" or a "swindler") that automatically constitute libel.

**Libertarian theory**: The assumption that all human beings are rational decision makers and that governments exist to serve the individual.

**Limited partnership**: Method of movie financing in which a number of investors put up a specified amount of money for a film.

**Machine-assisted interpersonal communication**: A method of communication involving one or more persons and a mechanical device (or devices) with one or more receivers.

**Macroanalysis**: A sociological perspective that considers the functions performed by a system (e.g., mass media) for the entire society.

**Magazine**: Printed publication that contains an assortment of materials that appears on a regular basis.

**Mainstreaming**: In cultivation analysis, the tendency of differences to disappear among heavy-TV-viewing people, apparently because of cultural and social factors.

**Management by objectives (MBO)**: Management

technique that sets observable, measurable goals for an organization to achieve.

**Marketing**: Developing, pricing, distributing, and promoting an idea, a good, or a service.

**Mass communication**: The process by which a complex organization, with the aid of one or more machines, produces and transmits public messages that are directed at large, heterogeneous, and scattered audiences.

**Mass media**: The channels and the institutions of mass communication.

**Meaning**: The interpretation an audience makes of text.

**Media buying service**: An organization that specializes in buying media time to resell to advertisers.

**Mediamark Research Inc. (MRI)**: Company that measures magazine readership.

**Media vehicle**: A single component of a mass medium, for example, a newspaper or TV network.

**Message**: The actual physical product in the communication process that the source encodes.

**Message research**: Pretesting messages in an ad campaign.

**Microanalysis**: A sociological perspective that considers the functions performed by a system (e.g., mass media) for the individual.

**Modem**: Device that allows computers to communicate via phone lines.

**Network**: An organization composed of interconnecting broadcasting stations that cuts costs by airing the same programs.

**Newsgroups**: Section of the Internet devoted to message boards that are organized according to topic.

**Newshole**: The amount of space available each day in a newspaper for news.

**Nickelodeon**: A popular name for the many penny arcades and amusement centers that emerged around the beginning of the 20th century and specialized in recordings and film.

**Noncommercial television**: Television programs broadcast by those stations whose income is derived from sources other than the sale of advertising time.

**Ombudsperson**: An individual in a media organization assigned to handle complaints from audience members.

**One-stops**: Individuals who sell records to retail stores and jukebox operators who are not in a position to buy directly from the record company.

**Opaid circulation**: A type of circulation in which the reader must purchase a magazine through a subscription or at a newsstand.

**Panel study**: A research method in which data are collected from the same individuals at different points in time.

**Pass-along audience**: That portion of a magazine's total audience composed of individuals who pick up copies of a magazine while at the doctor's office, at work, while traveling, and so on.

**Persistence of vision**: Quality of the human eye that enables it to retain an image for a split second after the image has disappeared.

**Phonograph**: A "talking machine" developed by Thomas Edison in the late 1870s; the hand-cranked device preserved sound on a tinfoil-wrapped cylinder.

**Photojournalism**: Journalism in which written text is secondary to photographs in news stories.

**Positioning**: In advertising, stressing the unique selling point of a product or service to differentiate it from the competition.

**Primary audience**: That portion of a magazine's total audience made up of subscribers or those who buy it at the newsstand.

**Primary demand ad**: Advertisement that promotes a specific product category, such as milk.

**Prominence**: News value that stresses the importance of the person involved in the event.

**Public Broadcasting Act of 1967**: Congressional act that established the Public Broadcasting Service.

**Rack jobbers**: Individuals who service record racks located in variety and large department stores by choosing the records to be sold in each location.

**Rate base**: Number of buyers guaranteed by a magazine and used to compute advertising rates.

**Rating**: The ratio of listeners to a particular radio station to all people in the market; the ratio of viewers of a particular TV program to the number of households in the market equipped with TV.

**Receiver**: The target of the message in the communication process.

**Reinforcement**: Support of existing attitudes and opinions by certain messages.

**Resonance**: In cultivation analysis, the situation in which a respondent's life experiences are reinforced by what is seen on TV, thus reinforcing the effect of TV content.

**Rough layout**: Early version of a print ad.

**Satellite news gathering (SNG)**: Using specially equipped vans and trucks to transmit live stories from any location via satellite.

**Sedition Act**: Act of Congress passed in the late 1790s that made it a crime to write anything "false, scandalous or malicious" about the U.S. government or Congress; it was used to curb press criticism of government policies.

**Selective demand ad**: Ad that stresses a particular brand.

**Self-determination**: Ethical principle that states that human beings deserve respect for their decisions.

**Share of the audience**: The ratio of listeners to a particular radio station to the total number of listeners in the market; the ratio of the number of households watching a particular TV program to the number of households watching TV at that time.

**Shield laws**: Legislation that defines the rights of a reporter to protect sources.

**Slander**: Spoken defamation. (In many states, if a defamatory statement is broadcast, it is considered libel, even though technically the words are not written. Libel is considered more harmful and usually carries more serious penalties than does slander.)

**Sliding scale**: An arrangement between a motion picture exhibitor and a distributor that details how much box office revenue will be kept by the movie theater.

**Socialization**: The ways an individual comes to adopt the behavior and values of a group.

**Social responsibility theory**: The belief that the press has a responsibility to preserve democracy by properly informing the public and by responding to society's needs.

**Social utility**: The media function that addresses an individual's need to affiliate with family, friends, and others in society.

**Soft news**: Features that rely on human interest for their news value.

**Source**: Person who initiates communication.

**Spam**: The electronic equivalent of junk mail.

**Status conferral**: A process by which media attention bestows a degree of prominence on certain issues or individuals.

**Stimulation theory**: A theory that suggests viewing violence will actually stimulate an individual to behave more violently.

**Storyboard**: A series of drawings depicting the key scenes in a TV ad.

**Strategic planning**: Management technique that sets long-range, general goals.

**Streaming video**: Method of sending TV over the Internet.

**Subsidiary rights**: Rights given by a publisher to others, allowing them to reproduce certain content.

**Surveillance**: The news and information function of the mass media.

**Survey**: A technique of gathering data that typically uses a questionnaire.

**Tabloid**: A heavily illustrated publication usually half the size of a normal newspaper page.

**Tactical planning**: Management technique that sets short-range, specific goals.

**Target audience**: In advertising, the segment of the population for whom the product or service has an appeal.

**Technological determinism**: The theory that contends technology drives historical change.

**Telecommunications Act of 1996**: Major revision of U.S. communication laws that affected broadcasting, cable, and telephone industries.

**Text**: Object of analysis in the critical/cultural approach.

**Timeliness**: News value that stresses when an event occurred.

**Time shifting**: Recording programs and playing them back at times other than when they were aired.

**Tracking studies**: Study that examines how ads perform during or after a campaign.

**Trespass**: Illegal entry onto another's property.

**UHF**: The ultra-high-frequency band of the electromagnetic spectrum; channels 14 through 69 on the TV set.

**Underground press**: A type of specialized reporting that emerged in the mid- to late 1960s, with emphasis on politically liberal news and opinion, and cultural topics such as music, art, and film.

**Utility**: Ethical principle that stresses the greatest good for the greatest number.

**Variety**: The entertainment industry trade publication.

**V-Chip**: A device installed in a TV set that restricts the reception of violent or objectionable material.

**Veil of ignorance**: Ethical principle that argues that everyone should be treated equally.

**VHF**: The very-high-frequency band of the electromagnetic spectrum; channels 2 through 13 on the TV set.

**Web page**: A hypertext page contained within a website.

**Website**: A set of hypertext pages linked to each other that contain information about a common topic.

**World Wide Web (WWW)**: A network of information sources that uses hypertext to link one piece of information to another.

**Yellow journalism**: Sensationalized journalism, appearing during the 1890s, noted for its emphasis on sex, murder, popularized medicine, pseudoscience, self-promotion, and human-interest stories.

Pearce, W.B. and Cronen V.E. 1980, *Communication, Action and Meaning,* New York, Praeger Press.

Potter, Geoff (1981), "Satellite-based Distance Education: Problems and Solutions", paper presented to RSDTA, Penang (Malaysia).

Rogers E.M. and Svennings L. 1969, *Modernisation among Peasants the Impact of Communications,* New York, Holt Rinehart and Winston.

Schramm Wilbur 1964, *Mass Communication and National Development,* Stanford, Stanford University Press.

Singh, Kusum Jitendra, *Gandhi and Mao as Communicators: A Comparative Study of Practice and Theory*, unpublished dissertation, University of Philadelphia, 1976.

Singh, Kusum Jitendra and Bertram Gross 1979, Challenges of Communication for Rural Reconstruction, *Media Asia* 6(1) 2-13.

Tolumin S. 1968, *Concepts and Explanation of Human Behaviour* In. T. Mischel (Ed) *Human Action,* Academic Press, New York.

Watzlawick Paul, *How Real is Real,* New York Random House, 1976.

# Index


**A**

A-B-X model, 92

Adam Smith, 58

Adler, M.K., 201

American Revolution, 58

Anglo-Saxon tribals, 50

Aristotle, 18

Arnheim, 133

Arousal, 88

Attitude and communication, 73

Audience, 6

Audio-visual communication, 185

uses and merits, 187

Audio-visual revolution, 176-213

Australia, 123

Authoritarian, 48

**B**

BCF, 32, 33

Bennett, James Gordon, 61, 63

Bill of Rights, 58

Bordenare, 20

Bowen, 162

Breed, Warren, 151, 152

British Association, 143

British Council, 172

Broadcasting, 230

Brown, 113

**C**

CAD, 203

Callender, JT, 56, 57, 59

CAM, 203

Circular concept, 22

Clark, JM, 161

Code systems, 80

Coke, Sir Edward, 50

Communication,

and information, 24

and perception, 74

categories, 24

concept of, 3

effects, 12

feedback in interpersonal, 17
functional, 25
geographic, 26
media of, 117
networks, 35
objective, 7
paradigms, 18
Communications revolution, 121-147
Competence, 31
Computer communication language, 209
Computer, 200
types of, 204
Cultural uniformity, 46

**D**

Davies, Haydn, 158, 159

**E**

Education, 234
EMMS, 220 221, 222
Etiquettes, 29

**F**

Festinger, Leen, 92
Francis, Clarence, 162
Freedom of Press, 168

**G**

Gagne, 102, 104, 113, 114, 120
Gestaltists, 87
Greeley, 160
Gross, 21
Grunig, 21

**H**

Harris, 34
Hoban, 117
Hussain, 214, 218
Hutchins Commission, 104

**I**

Iconicity, 83
*Iliad*, 135, 136
Information,
and communication network, 229
Technology, 232, 233
Inkeles, Alexander, 137

**J**

Jackson, Jay, 95
James, 107
Joncich, 98
Journalistic behaviour, criticism of, 173
Journalists, behavioural patterns of, 152

**K**

Kanter, Jerome, 215
Katz, 19
Kelly, George, 93
Kincaid, 19
Krampen, 81

**L**

Lasswell, 18, 71

Learning, 113

Lowry, 32

**M**

Marconi, 143

Mass communication, 1-42
- and MIS, 214-238
- basic elements, 6
- definition, 1,
- in democracy, 51
- major functions, 26
- models, 70
- nature of, 42-68
- organization, 28
- role of, 97
- theoretical approaches to, 69-

Mass Communicators,
- professional organization of, 148-175
- professional principles, 154
- staff training and discipline, 150

Mass line concept, 22

Mass media, 76, 95
- feedback in, 15

Mass readership,
- discovery of, 59

Mead, 17

Messages, 11, 75
- systems, 79

Miller, 80

MIS, definitions, 214-15

MuLuhan, Marshall, 86, 87, 137, 138

**N**

*National Gazette,* 56

Nazareth, 64

New Zealand, 123

Newcomb, 92

**O**

Osgood, 90, 91, 92

**P**

Pearce, 2, 4, 30, 33

Plato, 134

Press, professional council of, 171

Professionalism, 155

**R**

Receiver systems, 87

Renaissance, 145

Richards, I.A., 135, 136

Rogers, Everett, 96

Rokeach, Milton, 92, 93

Royal Commission on the Press in England, 157

**S**

Schramm, Wilbur, 18

Semantic space, 91

Shannon, 73, 83
Singh, K., 2
Skill development, 27
S-M-C-R model, 75, 93
Social organization, 46
Socrates, 134, 135
South Pacific, 123
S-R connections, 101
Stewart, A.T., 162
Symbol circulation concept, 20

**T**

Teleconferencing, 223
Telelecture, 227

**U**

United States Office of Education, 125

**V**

Verbal chains, 101
Visual aids,
- demerits, 184
- guidelines, for using, 181
- types of, 178
- major advantages, 182

Visual communication, 176, 186

**W**

Wittrock, 114